Living

Also by Jack Dominian:

Let's Make Love
One Like Us

Living Love

RESTORING HOPE IN THE CHURCH

JACK DOMINIAN

DARTON·LONGMAN + TODD

First published in 2004 by
Darton, Longman and Todd Ltd
1 Spencer Court
140–142 Wandsworth High Street
London SW18 4JJ

ISBN 0 232 52515 3

A catalogue record for this book is available from the British Library.

Phototypeset in 9.5/13pt Utopia by Intype Libra Ltd
Printed and bound in Great Britain by CPI Bath, Bath

Contents

Contents

Part Four: The Wider Family

Preface

This book about my Christianity, my Catholicism and my work would not have happened without a crucial episode in my life. In 1945, aged 16, I was on retreat with the Jesuits in Birmingham, and the retreat master asked me what I wanted to do when I left school. I replied that I wanted to become a psychiatrist. His face fell and, wagging his finger, he warned me that this would be the quickest way to lose my faith and my soul. I did not know then that my polite rejection of his admonishment was in response to a call from God that drew me towards my true vocation, and that my initial shift from infantile obedience to mature commitment had started me on a life-long path of loyal dissent. I now know that if I had not become a psychiatrist I would certainly have lost my faith and would have been prevented from serving Christ in the Church I love.

All my adult life I have been preoccupied with the subject of human love, living, unpacking, clarifying and writing about it in over 25 books from *Christian Marriage*[1] in 1967 to *Let's Make Love*[2] in 2002. This book expands my observations and conclusions to date. It is not written in any spirit of pride but in thanksgiving to God for giving me the years I needed to do this work.

I have learned everything I know about love from my wife, in whose presence I and many others have the privilege of experiencing the unconditional love of God.

Introduction

As with all my books, this one comes from the particular background of my Roman Catholic faith, but is addressed to the whole Christian community. This ecumenical approach has been a part of my writing for the last forty years, and is now particularly in sympathy with the growing awareness that Christians need to recognise that element of divine truth that is to be found in all religions. Although we must remain loyal to our individual traditions, Christians should also aim to reduce the scandal of divisions and to work hard for Christian unity.

We live in a time of transition when the certainties of the past are melting and society has, to a large extent, given up the religious practices focused on the local parish church which sustained it for centuries. Nevertheless, society remains spiritually hungry and awaits a renewal that it can neither see nor find in its experience of the traditional Churches.

I began to write this book at the beginning of the year 2003 – a year that saw the Roman Catholic Church preoccupied with the problem of priests acting as sexual predators and the resulting widespread scandal. While not trying to reduce by one iota the importance of the subject, it seems to me this is a typical displacement, shifting the Church's focus onto a peripheral issue rather than dealing with the central problem. In my view all the Churches recognise the decline of traditional Christian practices, but neither realise nor appreciate that we are witnessing the end of an era. We need to place Christianity in a radical new perspective, but all we are doing is chasing our tails with evangelising efforts that are clearly failing and are bound to fail because they are based on a type of religious thinking that is largely obsolete.

One of the aims of this book is to demonstrate the inadequacy of liturgical practices mainly led by the clergy and focused around the local church building. I suggest that one way forward is to make a spiritual shift away from the local church building and into the home and the community, with lay people as the Church's principal agents. We need to stop being mesmerised by the ideal of love, and make the living practice of loving the centre of Christian life. I visualise retaining the traditional church practices clothed in orthodox, liturgical, prayerful and sacramental life, underpinned by sensitive clerical participation as at present, but coupled with and expanded through a living community based on relationships of marriage, kinship and friendship and focused on feelings, emotions and experience. Above all, the Church should live with a spirituality of love at the centre and law at the periphery.

To put these ideas into practice we need to unpack their various elements, and in particular to look at the centrality of love in the Christian life. This book will ask questions about traditional religious practices and address the reasons for their decline in psychological terms. One feature about which there is a consensus is that, while there is a decline in traditional religious practices and an increasing mistrust of the Churches, a genuine spiritual hunger is now emerging in society. The most serious indictment that can be made against all the mainstream Churches is their inability to respond positively and with imagination to this challenge. I believe that historians of the future will find this particular failing the greatest deficiency of our Churches today.

In my view the possible reasons for the decline of the traditional Churches, and particularly the Roman Catholic Church, include:

- the growing maturity and autonomy of the laity
- the rejection of traditional authority in the form of blind submission
- the structure of the Church
- the issue of sexuality
- the difficulty of finding the presence of God in prayer, the liturgy and the Sacraments and
- the response of theology in its balance between philosophy and psychology.

These subjects will be tackled in the first part of this book and intermittently throughout. The second part will be devoted to a description and examination of the concept of love so often referred to in Christian life but so rarely actually lived in practice. In the third and fourth parts I shall cover love within marriage, the upbringing of children, kinship, friendship, singleness, work and loving ourselves and our neighbours.

One of my themes will be that, while Christianity recognises emotion, it has emphasised the intellect, at least in its predominant theologies. While acknowledging the transcendent in liturgy and prayer, it has alienated itself from the immanent presence of God in ordinary experiences based on relationships. Ours is an age that has brought relationship to the forefront, and our theology needs to rely primarily on understanding the inner world of relationships of love, as demonstrated by the Trinity. Instead, our religion has been underpinned by philosophical, intellectual and abstract ideas, and this has encouraged a faith based on belief and dogma rather than on living experience and love. From the earliest centuries, this pattern has reinforced the monastic and clerical state while marginalising the laity. We are now facing a conscious or unconscious desire for the laity and their life to be seen as the centre of the Church's life, where God is to be found.

I would like to emphasise that this is not another example of the historically recurrent priest-bashing. The priest has his, and maybe increasingly her, essential place. There is a decline in the number of clergy in most denominations and, since the Second Vatican Council, a striving to recover and find afresh the dignity and importance of the laity. In my opinion, one of the reasons for the current frustration, hurt and disappointment in the lay community has been the failure to implement the Council's vision in the last 25 years.

I believe that the reduction of church attendance and the fact that society is in a period of transition in which it does not trust all institutions, but remains spiritually alive, is the main challenge the Churches now face. In this book I want to find or at least begin to point to one or several routes that will satisfy this spiritual hunger. My first aim is to suggest one answer, namely to focus on life, lived in relationships based on love and informed by what we have learned from dynamic psychology over the past hundred years. My second is to analyse the most difficult subject in the world, namely love, and to remind ourselves that, according to St John, 'God is love' (1 John 4:8). Finally, I want to assert that, if we are not focused on love, we shall fail in our quest to evangelise the world.

Part One

_____

The Church Today

Chapter 1

The Decline of the Traditional Churches

My opening chapter looks at some statistics which put flesh on the bones of something we all know, namely that traditional religious adherence has declined in Western society. The traditional Churches, although aware of the drop in numbers and practice, are trying to revive a flagging religious interest by evangelisation efforts which, with a few exceptions such as the Alpha courses or the work of individual charismatic leaders, are failing. I boldly state that they will continue to fail because they ignore the fundamental issue of what is needed, and use the very methods that are in themselves the factors alienating people. Traditional evangelisation aims to bring people back to the Church through liturgy, prayer and the Sacraments. Apart from prayer, these are the very practices from which people are fleeing. I believe that the Churches are not trusted and that, while the founder of Christianity remains immensely significant, the Churches, who have the task of proclaiming the Good News, have managed to lose their significance.

Although statistics are boring and I will keep them to a very minimum, they provide pointers to historical trends: in other words, they are telling us in which direction we are going. Without any shadow of doubt, the most prominent marker of religious life in the Roman Catholic tradition is Sunday Mass attendance. In the United Kingdom, the weekly numbers peaked in 1964 at 2,114,219 but by 1998 had nearly halved to 1,086,268.[1] We do not really need these figures to draw our own conclusions – one look at our churches on Sunday shows an aged population attending and a virtual absence of young people. The loss of young people is particularly serious. The optimists assert that non-attendance is a temporary phenomenon of youth and that they will return when they are older, when they get married or when they have children. So far there is no evidence for this optimism, and, if the absence of the young today persists, our churches will be empty in a few decades.

Casting a brief look at attendances in other denominations, in 1957 55 per cent of the population attended the Church of England. By 1990 this had declined to 40 per cent, and by 2000 the numbers had fallen still further to 25 per cent. Similar declines were shown for Baptists, Methodists, Pentecostals and Nonconformists.[2]

Returning to the Roman Catholic Church, the Sacraments, particularly the Eucharist, are the central responsibility of the priest. Every Catholic is aware of the falling numbers of priests, their increasing age, and the lack of men offering themselves for ordination. On top of all this, the recent sexual scandals all add up to a picture of woe. The number of priests showed a peak in England and Wales of 7,714 in 1964. By 1997 there were 5,712, a number that has further declined in the last six years. Ordinations peaked in 1964 at 230; by 1996 there were only 119.[3] Seminaries are closing and to keep them functioning lay people are attending to obtain degrees in theology. This indicates that theology is no longer the exclusive province of the priesthood, and lays the foundations for a future when the laity will be as well informed and equipped to contribute to theology as the priest.

Turning to the other Sacraments, in Christianity Baptism is crucial as it incorporates us into the life of Christ. Once again, in 1964 there were 137,673 Baptisms in England and Wales. In 1977 the numbers had dropped to 67,364.[4] Confessions, once very popular, have now become virtually non-existent.

As the book unfolds, it will be seen how crucial marriage and the family are for the experience of love. Secular statistics show that marriage is declining in popularity in Britain. Marriages celebrated in church have dropped from a peak in 1964 of 45,592 to 14,705 in 1997.[5] In the framework of this book, married life, lived in and through love, will be shown to be the central factor of experiencing a life of love.

In my youth the Catholic Church lived life inside a fortress, inward-looking and very protective of its special identity. In those days those converting to the Catholic faith were seen as receiving an accolade, but conversions peaked in 1964 with 12,348; in 1997 there were only 5,089.[6] Taken as a whole, the figures make gloomy reading and indeed the article from which they were taken was headed 'Where have all the Catholics gone?'.

In the midst of all this statistical gloom, there is one bright feature, the presence of Catholic schools where numbers have remained steady and whose educational style has moved away from learning the faith by rote to living and participating in love, allowing openness and freedom to ask questions with frank answers as a response.

The USA

One of my most persistent concerns, expressed in numerous letters to the *Tablet*, is the current haemorrhage away from the Church of young and slightly older Catholics. Their non-adherence to traditional sexual teaching and challenges to the Church's authority are deeply significant, given that this group will form the next generation of Catholics.

A remarkable book published in the USA in 2003 appears to confirm my fears. In *The Coming Catholic Church*[7] the young adults surveyed are aged between 20 and 39, roughly overlapping the present pontificate. They represent nearly 40 per cent of the Catholic population of the United States and one third of Catholics who are effectively disconnected from the Church. Some 30–40 per cent of these young Catholics have never been confirmed and the number rises to 60 or 70 per cent among the Latinos. Only 10 per cent of those surveyed accepted all of the Vatican's pronouncements of faith, with the rest picking and choosing or subscribing to 'cafeteria' Catholicism. As the authors say, 'the demise of religious traditions is about the loss of the young, not the death of the old.'[8]

Twenty-seven per cent of these young people attend Mass weekly, a reduction from 42 per cent for the generation which came of age during the Second Vatican Council. They are less likely to consider obedience to Church moral teachings as central to faith (in sexual matters in particular) and they are more likely than the older generation to accept homosexuals in the Church and to support the idea of married and women priests.

In a separate section, the book suggests that the backbone of Catholic life was previously formed by people between the age of 25 and 45, and makes the point that: 'On most levels of the Church today, the leadership is still held by that same group – not the same age group but the same people now 20–30 years older.'[9] This coincides with my own observations as I lecture up and down the country – the majority of people in the audience are aged 50 years or over, with a scarcity of young people. In other words, younger Catholics are not involved in the structures of the Church and feel they have no voice and no stake in it. The book challenges us to:

> ... be honest and admit that most young Catholics, even into their 30s, are only semi-practising or non-practising. That does not mean they have abandoned God or been abandoned by God ... They are waiting for a credible, believable Church, a Church that addresses real life issues.[10]

This confirms my view expressed later on that the Vatican, as far as millions of young people are concerned, is talking to itself.

A wider survey of the whole Catholic community in the USA in 1999, charting responses going back to 1987, found a steady erosion of institutional loyalty. Of the six elements the researchers listed as integral to Catholic identity, the 'teaching authority claimed by the Vatican' was last on the list in 1999, with just 42 per cent of the Catholics surveyed agreeing it was 'very important'. The study goes on to record similar trends on abortion, on marriage, and on who had the final moral authority, church leaders or individuals, with the answer being in favour of the latter. As far as priestly presence is concerned, in 1965 there were 549 parishes in the USA without a resident priest. In 2002, this figure had risen to nearly 3,000.

These statistics point to an overall situation in Britain, the USA and, as we shall see, in Canada, which is a cause for severe concern. There are conservative Catholic leaders who express a preference for a remnant of traditional Catholics, however small their number. The sad fact is that this remnant comes from an older generation which is dying out and, in a few decades, unless the Church in its current form changes radically, even this remnant will not exist.

Canada[11]

Roman Catholicism is the largest religious denomination in Canada with just under 12.8 million members. Between 1991 and 2001 the number of Roman Catholics slightly increased, but this increase is accompanied by a national attendance in all denominations that has fallen dramatically across the country over the past 15 years. Nationally only 20 per cent of individuals aged 15 and over attended religious services on a weekly basis, compared with 28 per cent in 1986. The general decline can be seen from a Gallup poll conducted in 1945 which found that some 60 per cent of Canadians reported weekly attendance at religious services. More specifically, in Quebec, where Roman Catholics constituted about 95 per cent of the population, nine out of ten people claimed weekly attendance, presumably at Mass. These high numbers continued right up until the 1960s. Then came the steady drop also seen in Britain, with weekly attendance in Quebec dropping to 28 per cent by 1990.

In addition to the decline in attendance, there was growing disenchantment with the Church, with an increasing awareness of hypocrisy and a growing sense of disbelief. R. W. Bibby makes the same observations that we have previously seen in the USA, that religious groups were made up of a high proportion of older members.[12] The decline across Canada of all religions, including Roman Catholicism, is shown by the fact that in 1984, 23 per cent of the country's 15–19-year-olds were attending church on a weekly basis: by 1992 the figure had fallen to 18 per cent. As in the USA, the most involved people were those aged 55 or over.

My own serious concerns about the haemorrhaging Roman Catholic Church are underlined by the projected figures for weekly attendance at Mass. These are predicted to fall from 1.2 million in 1993 to about 600,000 in 2015 in Quebec. Another frightening statistic for the whole of Canada's Roman Catholic population, now no longer a projected figure but an actual measurement, is that in 1956, 83 per cent attended weekly Mass and that by 2000 the figure had dropped to 26 per cent. These devastating figures become more poignant when broken down into age groups. The 18–34 age group's weekly attendance was 12 per cent, rising to 38 per cent in the over 55s. Paradoxically, as we have seen in Britain and the USA, between

1985 and 2000 81 per cent of the whole population of Canada expressed a belief in God.

So far the figures show similar trends to those in Britain and the USA, namely a variable but serious decline in church attendance, especially among the young, with church attendance being buoyed up by older age groups. As in the USA, the hope of the conservative minority that a remnant of loyal, obedient Catholics will sustain the Church is a sheer fantasy, as the older group is not being replaced by the young.

A study by the publishers, Novalis, paints an even more serious picture. In 1973 there were 8,222 diocesan priests, but by 2003 the number had dropped to 5,666 and it can be presumed that this is an ageing population. The numbers of priests within religious orders dropped from 5,736 to 3,320 and the number of sisters from 44,006 to 22,539.

The Novalis study also cited data from a survey conducted by Canadian Press and Leger Marketing two months prior to the arrival of the Pope in Canada for the 2002 World Youth Day events in Toronto. This survey focused more clearly on the inner life of the Roman Catholic Church, and particularly on the views of the people of God on the very conservative John Paul II. In the survey, those very interested in him measured about 10 per cent, those somewhat inter-ested 27 per cent, those not very interested 21 per cent, and those not interested at all nearly 40 per cent. According to the survey, the last two groups together comprise nearly 60 per cent of the Catholic Church in Canada. Clerical celibacy is not at all well supported in Canada and indeed 52 per cent of those surveyed blame the vow of celibacy as the major cause of sexual abuse by the clergy, and 74 per cent thought that many doctrines were out of date. This inner picture of the Church shows that Catholic Canadians practise their weekly Mass attendance much less. They still identify with Roman Catholi-cism but have serious difficulties with the present pontiff and his conservative agenda.

Finally, as in Britain and the USA, R. W. Bibby shows that a spiritual hunger remains. This makes him optimistic about the future, but clearly this needs to be a profoundly different future. He feels that 'there is good reason to believe that spiritual opportunity continues to exist in the early years of the twenty-first century',[13] but adds that he is not confident about the established Churches, not only the Roman Catholic Church, as they are: 'Let us be brutally honest . . . Canadians may be hungry for the gods but that is hardly to say they are hungering for the Churches.'[14] This echoes what is happening in Britain where there is a sense of saying 'Yes' to God and 'No' to the Churches. Stark says, 'People continue to have some needs that only the gods can provide. The demand for a religion is constant.'[15]

Chapter 2

The Emergence of a New Spirituality

I finished the previous chapter with the notion that Western society was moving away from an acceptance of traditional religious rites, not to atheism but to a spirituality that is uncertain, tentative, lacking definition, but is definitely present. Sociologists claim that they see a decline in formal religion and, paradoxically, a rise in spiritual hunger, as a phenomenon widespread in the West.

How is this spirituality expressed? The first element of modern spirituality is a shift from conformity and blind obedience, particularly to figures of authority, to the inner authority of personal, mature judgement. For the Catholic Church this is a nightmare: its pyramidal, law-laden structure, historically clinging to hierarchical obedience to the Pope, bishops and priests, is ill-equipped to face this challenge. Jesus insisted on an egalitarian relationship of love in which he called his disciples friends. In the chapter on authority and autonomy, I shall deal with what this means for the Church, the Pope and the bishops and priests, and how they will have to adapt. At this point the conservative voice screams that the Church is not a democracy. I shall show that, although it is not a democracy, at its heart is individual conscience and accountability and for this to be truly authentic, the freedom of the individual must be respected and encouraged.

The second element of modern spirituality is the shift from organised traditional religious practices, taking place principally in a church building and focused around liturgy, the Sacraments and prayer, to a wider awareness of God. Central to this spirituality is

---

finding God everywhere[1] but particularly in people who are marginalised by society.

In the Oceanic Synod of Bishops, the principal groups of the marginalised were categorised as:

1. the mentally ill
2. Aids victims
3. drug addicts
4. the unemployed
5. victims of sexual abuse
6. the disabled
7. older people
8. refugees
9. single parents

The Church would have no quarrel with this list. It is familiar with material, educational and social poverty and part of the glory of all Christianity is its centuries of support for the disadvantaged through missionary, medical and educational work. Such poverty has not disappeared and the whole Christian community continues to respond to this day (for example, CAFOD, a principal Catholic agency, raised £26 million in 2002).

The Church now faces the dual task of loving the new poor and, vitally, including in this love those whose behaviour it does not approve of such as those having abortions, single mothers and the divorced. It needs to learn to disapprove of the acts but yet love the perpetrators. The Church must shift its emphasis from repeating condemnations *ad nauseam* towards supporting wounded human beings and working against the conditions that lead to marital break-down, divorce, abortion and euthanasia. Secular society has to see that the Gospel of love is not for the denominationally elite but for everyone.

The heart of the Gospel is the promotion of love and, both in encyclicals and Magisterium statements, the Church should avoid using criticism and condemnation and move to affirming the Gospel positively, not only to Christians but also to the world. In love we must recognise the qualities of mercy and compassion even if we do not always agree with the methods of providing relief. In matters such as abortion and euthanasia, Christianity is right in exalting the sanctity of life but wrong in attacking those who commit these acts. Sometimes the zeal of pro-life supporters hides their anger and hatred for their opponents. The only battle Christianity needs to join is the battle for prevention. Some conservatives see their sole job as to condemn what they do not approve of. Our Lord proclaimed that we should not see the mote in our neighbour's eye and ignore the beam in our own. All Churches have beams in their eyes and the Roman Catholic Church has a large one at present in the sexual outrages of some of its clergy. True, these priests are very few in number and the majority are not sexually corrupt but one is one too many.

The third element of emerging spirituality is concern about the protection of the environment, the extravagant use of limited resources and the fight against global warming and pollution. For many this concern is a new religion and Christianity has no quarrel with the aim of respecting God's creation, and promoting love of God's handiwork. To attack material greed is a very valid objective and the protestors at international meetings may be hidden martyrs.

The fourth element relates to healing. Many people feel that orthodox medicine has failed them, and turn to alternative therapies such as homoeopathy, special diets, aromatherapy, reflexology, crystal therapy and many others. To the orthodox believer and practitioner, this has nothing to do with spirituality, but the placebo effect of these treatments must be acknowledged, and, without further research, we cannot dismiss their intrinsic healing elements. What really matters is that those involved in these practices have a living faith that is part of their spirituality. In the same category are all the relaxation treatments including hypnotherapy, a whole variety of relaxation techniques using breathing exercises and yoga, which includes both relaxation and religious practices. Generally speaking, these practices involve some degree of contemplation and meditation.

The fifth element is a significant Western flirtation with Eastern religions, and an increase in following Buddhism, Hinduism and Islam. Eastern religions have an emphasis on inner peace and the inner emptiness that gives religious awareness which fascinates the West, and respect for these religions is important. These five elements underpin the new spirituality which is now emerging, although there are many other factors involved.

For the orthodox believer who only sees religion in the local church in liturgy, prayer and the Sacraments, the concepts I have just outlined come from a foreign world. They can be dismissed as attacks on orthodoxy or failures of obedience, and above all they can be lumped together as the product of the unhealthy mix that forms the New Age movement. This is a great mistake. Freedom of conscience, finding God in your environment and caring for it, and respecting other faiths are all vital ingredients of this emerging spirituality. Only when we recognise God in everyone and everything and move out from the confines of the local church building will we begin to connect spiritually with our neighbour. Orthodox beliefs focused on Christ must be defended, but not used as an excuse to dismiss the presence of God in the wider world. All this requires Christianity to make a shift from the intellect to the heart, from the abstract to experience, and from exclusive orthodoxy to spirituality as an entity with endless possibilities. We have been so conditioned and confined to the traditional orthodox sacred moments that we can be blind and deaf to the wider sacred moments that the Incarnation has brought within our orbit. For the orthodox the emerging spirituality can seem like a foreign language. For God there is no foreign language except to those who Jesus called the blind and the deaf.

Chapter 3

Redefining the Identity of the Church

The most serious problem facing the Churches today is that they are not trusted by the population at large. Archbishop Vincent Nichols of Birmingham has admitted that mistrust exists as a result of sexual scandals, but has not addressed society's wider mistrust of the Church. As we saw in the first chapter, this can be expressed simply as a 'Yes' to God and a 'No' to the Church. The rejection this implies is a very hard concept for the traditional Churches to accept and so they live, in psychological terms, in a world of fantasy and denial.

In the Catholic Church John Paul II has poured out encyclicals that, though intellectually brilliant, are couched in the language and style of a philosophical worldview which is foreign to nearly 99 per cent of ordinary Catholics. He is absolutely sincere in his repeated emphasis on personal morality and responsibility, indeed he insists that there is an absolute moral law and asserts the presence of absolute truth. However, this message is psychologically obscured by his personality, which can come across as authoritarian rather than authoritative. He is admired and respected but few can say he touches the heart of the world. He believes in courting opinion by confrontation but he is not in harmony with the society that he repeatedly criticises in the name of truth.

What he does not understand is that, while he is personally respected, the world and many Catholics are following their own agenda and pursuing their own truth, particularly in sexual matters. The Magisterium fails to appreciate the gulf between the official teaching and the life of the ordinary people, and it can take a catastrophe such as a sexual scandal to bring out the evils of secrecy, lack of openness and the protection of the priestly elite, and to uncover the hidden anger of ordinary people and their insistence on the accountability of their bishops. This is a new and unfamiliar world for many conservatively appointed bishops worldwide, requiring attentive listening to the laity, which has not happened in the past.

What really matters is that the decline of Church authority, its centuries-old authoritarian stance and the presence of sexual scandals together prevent the institutional Church from proclaiming God in and through the presence of Christ. Conservatives at all levels of the Church insist that all that is needed is obedience. They do not realise that the era of blind obedience is over, especially among the young, that trust and truth must be demonstrated and that the behaviour of the Pope, the bishops and the priests must be accountable. These thoughts seem very strange to conservative minds, but unless there is a powerful change the Church will continue to fail in its evangelising efforts. So we need to examine afresh what 'Church' means.

In the Church in which I grew up, and for traditional Catholics to this very day, 'Church' meant obedience to the Pope with his authority and infallibility. The Pope issued encyclicals and other documents which were to be obeyed, although they went largely unread as theological expertise was required to understand which were the most significant and how much obedience was required to each one. To the ordinary lay Catholic this was a totally obscure world, and even the ordinary priests and bishops needed help and clarification as to which instructions were to be taken seriously and which merely noted. Despite these hurdles, an overwhelming ethos of obedience to authority was the norm.

An emerging tendency in the post-Vatican II Church has been to distinguish between infallible and non-infallible teaching. This tendency has so alarmed Cardinal Ratzinger that repeated efforts have recently been made to re-establish obedience to all teaching, including the non-infallible. For the ordinary lay Catholic who still comes to church, the voice of the local bishop is important, though primarily to the older generations. But the expectation of obedience still prevails in the Catholic Church, and the current conservative administration is perturbed by the ever-growing emergence of autonomous, self-thinking, conscience-led Catholicism.

The Pope is clearly recognised as a person of supreme importance to the Church. He and the bishops all over the world form the Magisterium, which has the exclusive responsibility of teaching on faith and morals. Despite my very independent Catholic mind, I have no wish to see changes to the Church structure that would take one iota away from the significance and authority of the Magisterium. People need a leadership which proclaims the truth, and in some matters infallibly so. This is the glory of the Catholic Church, which claims that it continues to identify the truth as revealed by Christ. However, this magnificent ideal needs to be clearly understood. The truth that it proclaims must indeed be the truth. For this to be so, the experience of the Pope, bishops and priests is not enough, particularly in sexual matters. The laity are not seeking executive powers but to be consulted seriously, especially in matters that are their domain and where they have special experience. The Second Vatican Council insisted on the importance of the laity informing the Church. Newman proclaimed the need to consult the faithful. It should not take the catastrophe of priestly sexual scandal and bishops' resignations for the laity to be heard. Resignations in these circumstances are the result of practices dear to the Church such as secrecy, clerical protection and, in my opinion, sexual obscurantism, all of which weaken the authority and integrity of the Church.

The Pope and his fellow bishops rule and teach but, without being a democracy, the Church must listen and take heed of the laity, for it needs to reflect the truth that belongs to the whole Church and not just to a minority. While recognising the unity of Pope and bishops in their teaching role, there is always the danger of stressing the predilections of individual Popes. While I have no quarrel with the unilateral authority of the Pope, the gross neglect of collegial consultation as recommended by Vatican II is a severe indictment of the present situation and a problem for ecumenism. Clearly the Pope as the head of the Church needs a civil service, a group of Cardinals and bishops who head various congregations and advise the Pope, but it is widely recognised in the Church that the Curia, both historically and particularly at present with the ailing John Paul II, has wielded too much power.

The seat of government for the Church is in Rome. The central power of Rome as opposed to that held by national hierarchies is a source of tension and one that Vatican II wanted to address. Instead, under John Paul II and Cardinal Ratzinger, power has consolidated more and more in Rome. I appreciate the point that, without a strong and vigilant central authority, the Catholic Church fears disintegration, leading to a marked distrust of local hierarchies and the maturity and wisdom of the people of God. It goes without saying that this stranglehold in Rome is a great difficulty for Christian unity and an obstacle even for many Catholics.

Central to the concept of Church is the command of Christ to set up a community with a head, and the descendants of the Apostles as bishops to proclaim the centrality of Jesus as the Son of the Father, who, with the Spirit, forms the person of God. At the heart of this community is God who, according to St John, is love. The Church then spread to the whole world beyond Jerusalem, being nearly universal at the time of Constantine and its shaping by Roman law. The subsequent evolution of the Church has created a tension between the centrality of Rome, with authority wielded by the Pope and, for a long time, linked to secular rulers. At another level, the tension is between the proclamation of rules and the exercise of law, and the life of Christ lived through love. This tension between these two elements can prove both the strength and weakness of the Church, and I personally believe that it currently errs on the side of excessive emphasis on law at the expense of the understanding and practice of love.

When law, authority and obedience were central and largely adhered to, many could see the absurdities of the pre-Vatican II Church with its emphasis on eating of fish on Friday, infantile obedience to the clergy, attendance at Sunday Mass as a discipline rather than as a sacred event, and the significance of the people's physical presence in the church. Much importance was placed on whether we 'heard' Mass, and which parts of the Mass attendance satisfied the law, and this was coupled with a fear of sin, particularly sexual sin. The marks of being a Catholic in the church in which I grew up were not eating meat on Fridays, not using contraception and attending Sunday Mass as an obligation. This was all well meant, but new generations are rebelling against these constraints as they are growing up into mature Christians. Their focus is not on Latin, ritual and rules but on using their own language, understanding the

Scriptures, deepening their insight and reverence for the reality of Christ and sharing his life of grace, not as piped energy received in units but as a living reality of his life lived in love.

I have unhappily and reluctantly concluded that the pre-Vatican II Church which placed law at its centre and love at its periphery obscured rather than manifested Christ. The current gradual return to pre-Vatican II thinking is risking the same dangers and, however slight the shift, it sends shivers down the spines of those who appreciate what is at stake.

The pre-Vatican II Church I have described is largely what ordinary lay Catholics understood the Church to be. Conservative elements in the Church still try to resuscitate this picture, emphasising authority, law, obedience, fear and sin. This is of course a generalisation, but, as I shall show in subsequent chapters, there is a deep need in all of us, made up as we are of a combination of adult and child, to react as a child. This can be fed in an unhealthy way when we are told what to do and have authority taken from us (the 'Yes, Father', 'No, Father', 'What shall I do, Father?' syndrome). The Catholic Church is a magnificent worldwide organisation, but there is an inherent weakness in its structures which can lead it to infantalise its members. The Church of the future has to retain its vigour in defending the truth, but reduce infantile dependence and concentrate on encouraging the presence of Christ in everyday experiences of love in human relationships.

While I am highly critical of the past and aware of its contribution to the present decline of priests and church attendance, there is another factor which must be noted. The two world wars greatly perturbed contemporary theologians (who at this time were almost exclusively clerical). They questioned how these wars could start in a Europe dominated by Christianity and particularly by the Roman Catholic Church and started to examine the Church afresh. They perceived a body dominated by external structures and more concerned with the exercise of power and the preservation of the status quo than with her inner life as a community and the spirituality of her people: a Church seemingly deaf both to the persistent calls for conversion and reform, and the cries of a world seeking a simple explanation of Christ's programme of redemption.

In response, Pius XII issued an encyclical, *Mystici Corporis*, in

1943, reconciling the older emphasis on the Church's visible, institutional and societal aspects with the hunger for the rediscovered invisible, spiritual and mystical elements. The encyclical emphasised Christ, not the institutional aspect of the Church: in the words of the encyclical there was 'nothing more noble, more sublime, or more divine than the expression (of the Church) as the Mystical Body of Jesus Christ'.[1] Here at last the significance of Christ in the life of the Church was brought forward as a central image.

This anticipated Vatican II, not that any ordinary lay Catholic living in the 1940s would have been aware of it. The pulpit remained the centre of preaching moral theology, mostly Thomistic, with its emphasis on sin, punishment and hell, the dangers of sexuality and the importance of marrying a fellow Catholic and bringing up children in the Catholic faith. Christ and love had very little place in that pulpit. I know because I was in the congregation! Theologians both welcomed and criticised the encyclical because, both in 1943 and in 1950 in the encyclical *Humani Generis*, Pius XII identified the strict boundaries of the Catholic Church and, of course, the prevailing legalistic structures. Once again theologians asked questions: Where did the Church stand in relation to the world, to the nations, to other Christian communities and other religions? Was it appropriate for her to teach spiritual flight from the world and to discourage association with other religious communities? Some theologians wanted to emphasise inclusiveness with humanism, awareness of God in the world and the contribution of other religious communities rather than the exclusiveness of the Roman Catholic Church and the presence of the truth within the confines of her boundaries.

The bishops of Vatican II, responding to these criticisms, were in fact redefining the identity of the Church. They were aware of the tensions between what might generally be called the conservative and the progressive thinking of her various theologians. Despite persistent efforts by the conservatives, the Council favoured a progressive, more liberal identity. The Church now became the whole people of God, with a very welcome significance attached to the laity, ecumenism, the centrality of the Mass, a positive evaluation of sexuality, and an emphasis on love as the heart of the Church, with the personal and inter-personal encounter becoming more important than the Church's jurisdiction.

For the majority of the Church, the Council and its Pope were a breath of fresh air. But those who opposed its spirit did not go away. They have been much in evidence under John Paul II, who, whilst undoubtedly a brilliant mind, is an unconcealed conservative. The strict teachings of the Council are retained but its liberal, progressive spirit is severely restricted. This is shown by the failure of authentic collegiality, the appointment of conservative or 'safe' bishops and an ambivalence towards the laity, together with a preference for the clerical and religious if only through their canonisation. It is also shown in the perpetuation of an anachronistic sexual theology and the placing of conservative personalities in key posts, the ever-growing trend to exclusiveness rather than inclusiveness, the subtle but undoubted love affair with triumphalism and the obvious hostility to the world and its values.

One unconscious effect of the pontificate of John Paul II has been its divisive consequences for the Church. This has placed a heavy burden of frustration and disappointment on those who welcomed the spirit of Vatican II and leaves them with the appointment of a new Pope in the future as their only hope. This conservative Pope undoubtedly believes that restraining of the spirit of Vatican II is the right course for the Church. Sadly, during the last 25 years we have seen a large exodus from the Church by the laity, a severe reduction in priestly numbers and vocations and the acute haemorrhaging of young people away from the Church. John Paul II, the Magisterium and the Curia do not see the connection between the two. Indeed, in a strange way, some blame the Council for the exodus. Psychologically, we know that we see what we want to see and act according to our rigidly held personality traits.

Thankfully, many who have left the Church have not left God, as we shall see in the next chapter. The majority who follow Christ and celebrate the Eucharist do not disturb themselves with the wider issues, although, as parents, they are seriously confused and concerned by their children's non-participation in church life. They know that leaving the Church is no answer for them and in many small ways carry the spirit of Vatican II in their lives, forming a community of love, meeting their neighbour in ecumenism and helping the poor.

Within this large majority, there is still a noisy conservative minority which vehemently attacks those who loyally dissent. The latter do not depart but defend with all their energy the spirit of Vatican II, while praying for those who have left and their critics who remain.

Chapter 4

The Persistent Sense of God

The Church and its activities have traditionally been linked in most people's minds with a sense of God, expressed through God the Father, Jesus and the Holy Spirit as the embodiment of holiness. We have seen so far that attendance at church services has been greatly reduced, but that spirituality and belief in God remain high. The following figures, taken from the BBC *Soul of Britain* survey[1], help us to define this spirituality more clearly:

- In 1968 nearly 80 per cent of the population of Britain believed in God, and this had fallen to just over 60 per cent in 2000.
- In 1968 45 per cent of the population believed in a personal God (a core teaching of Christianity), and this had fallen to 25 per cent in 2000.
- In 1968 10 per cent of the population did not believe in God and this had risen to nearly 30 per cent in 2000.
- In 2000 nearly 70 per cent of the population believed in the soul.
- In 2000 50 per cent of the population believed in heaven, but only 30 per cent believed in hell.
- In 2000 nearly 70 per cent of the population believed in sin, but only 30 per cent believed in the Devil.

These figures generally show the persistence of a sense of God, but belief in a personal God has diminished. The word 'God' is problematic. What do we mean by God? I will begin with a brief review of philosophical, biblical and psychological understandings of God.

The philosophical concept of God started with Greek thought. Greek philosophers approached the sense of God through both polytheism and monotheism. God was conceived as an impersonal principle rather than a person: a principle of order, not of creation. In this view, God organises the world, but is not infinite, as infinity is allied to imperfection.

The Judaeo-Christian tradition, on the other hand, affirmed God as person, creator, omnipotent, infinite, perfect, and the source of all existence and value, and it was this sense of God that held sway until the Enlightenment.

A crucial aspect of the Enlightenment was the development and advance of science, and as a result the world has been powerfully influenced by the idea of scientific proof. Our contemporary minds are conditioned to ask, 'What is the evidence?' The conflict between science and religion is very much in evidence in the concept of God as a creator. Darwin undermined the biblical notion of creation in seven days. On the other hand, science, with its massive advances in understanding the origin of matter, is actively posing new questions: far from the mystery being eliminated, the more we discover, the more awestruck we are at the complexity and order of creation. Here science enhances, rather than diminishes the sense of God. However, it has also served to weaken the belief in the abstract, non-material world. People want to measure, see and touch. Science insists on these criteria but the truth extends beyond science.

The biblical sense of God is a concept of the invisible and the untouchable. It is presented as a mystery difficult to grasp. In 1 Kings 19:9, 11–13, we read:

> Elijah went into a cave and spent the night in it. Then he was told 'Go out and stand on the mountain before the Lord.' Then the Lord himself went by. There came a mighty wind, so strong it tore the mountain and shattered the rocks before the Lord. But the Lord was not in the wind. After the wind came an earthquake. But the Lord was not in the earthquake. After the earthquake came a fire, but the Lord was not in the fire. And after the fire came a gentle breeze, and when Elijah heard this he covered his face with his cloak and went out and stood at the entrance to the cave. (1 Kings 19:9, 11–13)

This scene when considered superficially is an obstacle to the

Christian concept of God being present in creation, but, looked at deeply, it supports the sense of the mystery of God.

Another concept of the Christian God that presents problems is the image of an all-powerful, perfect, loving God. How can such a God allow evil, pain and catastrophes? Christianity has no real satisfactory answer. We can say that pain, anxiety and suffering are warnings of danger against which we have to protect ourselves. We can say that a loving God also gives perfect freedom and allows evil. We can say that it is due to original sin, or as I like to understand it, original alienation, which is called a cop-out by ardent humanists. But none of these answers satisfies the paradox of a loving God who allows pain, suffering and destruction. That is why in Christianity, the answer is not just in reason, but in faith in the Cross.

A psychological root of atheism is the concept of humanity with its powerlessness projecting an imaginary sense of a God who does not exist. This was expressed very powerfully by Feuerbach in *The Essence of Christianity*.[2] Feuerbach's idea that mankind 'created' God was continued in the twentieth century by Freud, who postulated that we are born as helpless children and we project God the Father as an imaginary parental figure who is there to depend on and who will protect us. Finally, in economic terms, Marx saw religion as the opium of the people.

All the schools of thought that together see God as an external human projection do not seem to diminish the deep, enduring, internal human awareness and hunger for the divine. The God of the philosophers and Yahweh in the Old Testament is a God who exists 'out there'. There is also a sense of God on the 'inside', proposed by Jung as an archetype (a primordial image that appears in myths, legends and fairy tales). This God inside and within has been further postulated as a spiritual principle by Alastair Hardy, Professor of Zoology at Oxford. He proposed that religious experience involves a kind of awareness that has evolved through natural selection because of its survival value to the individual.[3]

Hardy's work has been extended by David Hay at the Centre for the Study of Human Relations at the University of Nottingham. Hay carried out surveys of religious and spiritual experiences among the British population and discovered in 1987 that 45 per cent had had such experiences. In 2000 some 55 per cent felt there was a patterning in their lives, 38 per cent had an awareness of the presence of God and awareness of prayers being answered, and 29 per cent were aware of a sacred presence in nature, with 25 per cent having an awareness of the dead and a similar figure for the awareness of an evil presence.[4]

The above description of the sense of God, from the Greek philosophers, through Judaeo-Christian tradition, to the psychology of Jung and the biology of Hardy and his colleagues, confirms the undefined but strong sense people have that there is something 'out there' or 'within'. This 'something' can be described as a carer or expressed in St John's concept that 'God is love' (1 John 4:16), giving, in Hardy's terms, a sense of guidance, strength, help and assistance. All those who positively affirm the sense of God express a living reality, captured most brilliantly by St Augustine's saying. 'You have made us for yourself and our heart is restless until it finds rest in you' (*Confessions* 1.1).

This is not a God who fills in gaps, despite the humanist belief that the Christian sense of God is an illusion waiting to be annihilated by the next leap of science. God is a psychological presence, not just a product of infantile dependence which is gradually being eliminated by the progress of autonomy, independence and the mastery of the environment, but a profound expression of a heart of love, as I stress in this book.

The combination of belief and a sense of God remains high. For most of Western Christianity's existence this concept of God has been described in terms of reason and intellect. This logic has in recent centuries met much of the philosophical challenge but the triumph of the sense of God as a call from the heart, however confused, continues despite the onslaught of science, the presence of evil and the scandals of Christian life.

Despite society's 'No' to the Churches and its 'Yes' to God, the Judaeo-Christian tradition has maintained that, although science asserts that God cannot be found in the human body alive or dead, the person is more than a body. That people believe in the presence of the soul and have a sense of God is affirmed in survey after survey. Nevertheless, the withdrawal from church attendance, which powerfully expresses belief, has to be taken seriously. It suggests that Churches at present are unwittingly masking God's Spirit, and in the next few chapters I shall examine briefly the reasons for this.

Chapter 5

Autonomy, Authority and Trust

Historically, until the Enlightenment, Christianity was the principal source of education for most people in Europe who could not read or write. The pulpit was the source of knowledge and the majority of people relied on the priest for wisdom and healing. The Church's authority rested on the belief that it was founded by Christ, and headed first by Peter and the apostles and later by the Pope and the bishops in a structure that continues to this very day.

The arrival of printing, the dissemination of information, the translation of the Bible into vernacular languages and the Reformation resulted in a considerable reduction of the Church's spiritual and secular authority. These changes, combined with the ascendancy of monarchical rulers, led to a tension between Church and State. Gradually the prince bishops' power faded, and the Church now has only a symbolic presence on secular territory in the Vatican in Rome.

As the Reformers advanced, the Catholic Church assumed a very defensive position. Spiritual orthodoxy became increasingly predominant and was defined in detail by the Council of Trent in 1545. A preoccupation with the Church's identity and authority culminated in the First Vatican Council's definition of papal infallibility in 1869, and during the next hundred years the Church became a fortress of authoritarianism, with power resting almost exclusively with the Pope, bishops and priests. For many people, this Church, with its strict rules, clear and absolute black and white moral theology and adherence to orthodox teaching and obedience was a source of security greatly admired both by its own adherents and by outsiders. This view of the Church was reassessed by the Second Vatican Council in the 1960s, which changed many things, to the infinite relief of much of the Church and the regret of some. I have already mentioned the tension and division in the Church under the present markedly conservative regime. I have also mentioned the large-scale haemorrhage of the young and not so young from church attendance during this papacy.

A current and predominant feature of our society is that a new autonomy is emerging in all age groups, but particularly among the young. Advances in education, science and political democracy have created an atmosphere of independence. People are much more well informed and are accustomed to making up their own minds, and authoritarian systems that attempt to think for people and demand unconditional obedience face difficulties. This growth of autonomy is complex, and is something the Catholic Church has found very difficult to acclimatise itself to, although it made a brilliant effort in the Second Vatican Council by placing conscience as the supreme arbiter of moral decisions. In the last 25 years, the Church has had no option but to accept the essentials of the Council but it has tried to erode their significance by insisting that the conscience must be an informed one. So John Paul II and the Curia have penned document after document clarifying the Council's teaching but emphasising the more conservative elements.

There is nothing wrong with having authoritative teaching and people do want clarity about what to believe and how to live their moral life. But, and it is a big but, nowadays they want to scrutinise very carefully what is taught and whether it rings true with their basic experiences. Abstract theology written in Latin does not connect with experience lived in everyday life. At the centre of this tension is the teaching on sexuality. I shall tackle this subject in the next chapter but the problem can be summarised succinctly, in that a great deal of the current teaching of the Church, particularly on contraception, is unacceptable to the majority of Catholics. So this teaching is ignored and autonomy is exercised, but not only in this area. The people of God are now becoming accustomed to determining their spiritual life in other areas, for example, by choosing the Sacrament of Communal Reconciliation rather than personal Confession.

What is the answer to this tendency to an autonomy which ignores what the Magisterium considers core teaching? I believe the present situation is highly unsatisfactory because, despite what the Magisterium thinks, its teaching is widely ignored and there is no point in the Church teaching with authority if it is not listened to: often it seems to be talking to itself.

One of the answers to this complex but unhappy situation is simply that, if the people of God are expected to believe in any teaching, then, whenever applicable, their own experience must be part of the input, particularly in matters where they are the experts, such as marriage, love and sexuality. This is very difficult for the Church, which is accustomed to relying on its celibate theologians, and to making decisions based on the thinking of a limited number of these theologians. The Church has to acknowledge two things: firstly that that experience is an authentic source of truth, and secondly that the laity are increasingly becoming far more theologically informed and articulate.

This leads to the subject of authority and obedience. The Church has been accustomed to being obeyed unconditionally and, even to this day, it exercises this authority where it has the power to do so, for example in seminaries, some higher institutions and universities, where professors and teachers can be fearful of expressing openly opinions other than those which are approved of from above. The result is conformity and obedience at a price. The first casualty is the truth, the second is outward compliance and inner defiance, and the third and most serious is that people vote with their feet. In my lifetime many outstanding priests have left the Church. There has also been a destructive habit of appointing bishops who are compliant and obedient, but who then inevitably find it very difficult to think for themselves and to initiate changes which they know their people want.

In the past the expected obedience has been generated simply by laying down the law. This is becoming more and more difficult, particularly with young people. For them, truth is something they need to be persuaded about and to see being adhered to by corporate consent. Those who find this approach unacceptable cry out about anarchy, but it is fundamentally about respect for human dignity. This is not easy for an authoritarian Church to take on board, although it is beginning to happen in schools and in other spheres of the life of the Church. This freedom and cooperation is more successful in schools than in parish appointments where authoritarian priests still exist, and parishes are sometimes turned upside down when a conservative regime replaces one based on Vatican II.

Here we need the greater consultation that is still singularly absent in the appointment of bishops and priests and, in the wider Church, genuine, not pseudo-collegiality. Having said all this, in the aftermath of the Second Vatican Council, much is happening in terms of collaborative ministry, involvement of the laity, adult religious formation, exposition of new ideas by the laity, increased status given to women and so on. Nevertheless, despite this growth among the laity, there is a paradox. Articles are written describing how difficult some priests find it to involve the laity and to invite initiatives and ideas from them, particularly if they are original and innovative. For a psychiatrist, this contradiction is perfectly comprehensible. In all of us there is a strong trait of dependence and a desire for a child-like obedience to authority. The Catholic Church has capitalised on these traits and has governed unconsciously by catering to these infantile needs. One of the real challenges is to promote maturity, and for those who rule to respect this maturity.

I accept absolutely the need for structures of authority in the Church. I think it is essential that a voice of authoritative teaching should exist and prevail because we all need the truth. I accept that the Church, the Magisterium and the Pope must speak on certain occasions with authority and rarely infallibly. What is putting people off all Churches and particularly the Catholic Church is that they are perceived as being authoritarian rather than authoritative. Although the Church is not a democracy but a hierarchy, it will have no choice but to apply democratic principles of listening to the voice of the people of God, discerning the truth, not in secrecy and through clerical cliques, but by being open and inclusive.

The present structure of the Curia is untenable. A Church governed by a Curia that operates in offices from 9 a.m. to 5 p.m. and is disconnected from the people it governs, cannot but restrain the Spirit who guides them. In the aftermath of Vatican II, tentative steps were made towards change but they never got very far and John Paul II finds the necessary changes not to his taste.

All conservatives (not just Roman Catholics) abhor change, and they are often rigid personalities. This is a psychological issue: change is threatening to security and demands personal and social alteration, which is always difficult. The very core of our inner world, our identity and its security, is threatened and changes are often vehemently resisted. The term 'liberal' is used as a term of opprobrium by a small minority of Catholics who hide behind support for authority, obedience and a current regime that thinks likewise. All this will be described as 'psychobabble' by those who believe that they are defending traditional truth. The Church wants to perpetuate its conservative structures of thought in the appointment of bishops but there is no way of evaluating their personalities and the traits they bring with them.

Catholic structures can also have huge advantages. A council can change overnight what the Church has taught for centuries, for example the change of the definition of marriage at the Second Vatican Council. There is no doubt that ultimately the Catholic Church has the means of discovering the truth and it rests on this claim.

In the meantime the current tension between conservatives and liberals is critical, because what is at stake is putting Catholics off from participating in the most vital Sacrament, the Eucharist. On the surface, the issue is about authority and obedience. In fact it is about facilitating or blocking the Spirit. Most people who are conservative are really protecting their human security. In fact, by opposing changes evoked in the spirit of Vatican II, they are applying the brake to intimacy with the life of God in the Eucharist and other Sacraments, the very life of grace.

I have focused on the life of the Catholic Church, as I know it best, but what I have outlined applies to all Christian denominations. Fundamentalism in the Protestant tradition, through adherence to the letter of the word of the Bible, fails to take note of the numerous scriptural studies that offer alternative explanations. This fundamental Protestant adherence has some similarities with the Roman Catholic Church's fanatical emphasis on obedience to authority. Catholics are afraid that Protestant autonomy makes belief and morality a menu of personal choice, and I know several Protestants who yearn for the discipline of the structure and homogeneity of the Catholic Church. I also know and have described above people's frustrations with John Paul II and the current regime.

Part of the decline of Christianity is caused by the scandal of its divisions and the lack of unanimity of moral teaching. Even more serious is society's mistrust of the Churches which are perceived as distant and alien from what people have come to be familiar with: the apparent reliability of science with its emphasis on the concrete, visible and touchable, and the psychological freedom of autonomy. Too often the Churches can appear to be like museums holding an irrelevant past in their rooms.

What they hold, however, is the sense of mystery, the sacred, the holy, and above all, the cement of life which is love. John XXIII expressed this, combining the holy with a sense of awe, mystery with profound clarity of what is true, and a framework of organisational reference with flexibility. In the United Kingdom, Cardinal Hume became the accepted symbol of holiness and the conscience of the nation.

The 'No' to Churches is also due to their love affair with bureaucracy and structure. People understand that there have to be visible structures in the Churches. But they desire what was shown in Jesus Christ, the presence of love, and it is my conviction that this is the only thing that will restore the integrity of all Christianity. People want to see holiness and, visible in it, love.

> God is love, and whoever remains in love remains in God, and God in him. (1 John 4:16)

Only when this profound psychological reality, which is at the heart of spiritual truth, is seen in the external life of the Church and lived in the internal life of its people will trust return, because it will reflect and echo the universal reality of life. In the present tension between conservatives and liberals (I hate the terms but they explain an aspect of the reality succinctly), change in the direction of the liberal spirit of Vatican II is inevitable. Why? Simply because what people want out of life is changing radically, at least in the West. The European Values Survey in 1981 and 1990 pointed to a growing emphasis, particularly in those aged under 50, on the following:

- personal autonomy and self-expression
- personal growth
- openness in public institutions
- participating in those decisions that affect people's lives

- self-reliance
- protest and an emphasis on human rights
- toleration of 'deviant' private morality, but intolerance of public behaviour which encroaches on the quality of common life.[1]

There is a limit to how much the conservative regime of the present can deviate from the prevailing ethos of the world outside. There are, of course, issues that it must take a stand on, but the democratic identity of being human is not one of them. The brake has been put on the Second Vatican Council, but not for long, for it is going in the same direction as the world we live in.

Chapter 6

Sexuality

One of the reasons why the Church in Western society is virtually ignored is that its language, interests and concerns are so often far removed from the living reality of ordinary people at home and at work. The Church's priorities are with the variety of liturgical expression that gives the Church its sense of identity. Freedom, choice and independence are not vital components of this identity. While the Church is energised by Scripture, teaching and prayer, it is the concrete, everyday moment that shapes the inner world of ordinary men and women. The Spirit is also part of this living world but there is a tension between the Spirit portrayed as a living but abstract reality and the material concreteness of everyday living.

The tension between the abstract dimension of the spiritual and the immediacy of technology, science and ordinary life is something that the Churches have to face. The challenge is to avoid dismissing everyday life as a product of secular materialism, and instead to recognise that ordinary, essential existence comes from and coincides with God, identifying the divine presence in the ordinary moment. Despite its best efforts, the parish church and its activities do not naturally and intimately relate to home and work. The two do not walk in the same direction.

This is precisely the problem with sexuality. From time immemorial its importance has been recognised but, since Freud, it is now appreciated that sexuality is an essential part of the personality, central to the very fabric of our being. This is light years away from how it is perceived in Christianity. In an age that recognises its importance, this contributes to a marked alienation from Christianity, particularly among the young. The media speaks and portrays one language and message and the Church another. The Church simply does not take sexuality seriously. When, for example, has there been an encyclical devoted to it? Even when it is considered, until recently the summary has been 'Yes' to sex for procreation, 'No' to sex for pleasure and, literally only in the last fifty years in all Churches, 'Yes' to love.

This shows how limited Christianity has been on the subject of sexuality. Its theology has been deeply flawed. It has substantially ignored the positive contribution of the Old Testament:

> This is why a man leaves his father and mother and becomes attached to his wife and they become one flesh. Now, both of them were naked, the man and his wife, but they felt no shame before each other. (Gen. 2:24–25)

'God saw all He had made and indeed it was very good' (Gen. 1:31), and the Song of Songs are among many other positive passages.

Christianity tended to ally sexuality with sin in the teaching of the early Fathers, culminating in the teaching of St Augustine whose emptying of its goodness was intimately linked with his own long-standing preoccupation with sex and pleasure.[1] Augustine's giant intellect has cast a shadow to this day both in the Roman Catholic and Reformed Churches, but if ever there was a negative psychological contribution dressed up as theology it was his. Luther followed the negativity of Augustine and so, for him, marriage was a medicine, a 'hospital for the sick'.[2]

Not knowing what to do with this powerful experience, and saddled with the erroneous convictions that sex and pleasure were a barrier to holiness, Western Christianity collectively turned to celibacy and the monastery as a fitting answer. The single state dedicated to God was commended both by Paul (1 Cor. 7:38) and by Jesus in the following passage:

> The disciples said to him, 'If that is how things are between husband and wife, it is advisable not to marry.' But he replied, 'It is not everyone who can accept what I have said, but only those to whom it is granted. There are eunuchs born so from their mother's womb, there are eunuchs made so by human agency and there are eunuchs who have made themselves so

for the sake of the kingdom of Heaven. Let any one accept this
who can.' (Matt. 19:10–12)

Part of the flawed tradition of the Catholic Church on sex once it
had made celibacy compulsory for the priesthood has been to fail to
distinguish between the priesthood and celibacy. It is much simpler
if you listen to Jesus and not to the negativity of Augustine and the
early Fathers. Some people want to be priests. Some people want to
be celibate. Jesus never said that the two should necessarily be
combined compulsorily. What has been and still is a serious and
confusing issue is that the dignity of the single state dedicated to God
is mixed up with the priesthood. Priesthood is sacred because priests
serve the Kingdom of God in a special way, not because they are
celibate.

A great deal of the distortion of compulsory celibacy, and some of
the recent scandals in the Catholic Church, have come about because
the Church is influenced by the negativity of its tradition on sex and
sees the goodness of the celibate priest in this tradition as something
positive rather than as an unconscious defence against sexuality's
threat to the holiness of the priest. As historians point out, the threat
of sexuality for the man is also linked with fear of women. The combination of a faulty tradition and fear of women makes the Catholic
Church extremely stubborn in changing laws about the priesthood
and marriage.

The link between Jesus, love, availability and the service of the
single state has never wholeheartedly penetrated the psyche of
the people of God. What has penetrated is the familiar 'no sex',
hence the current shock of the priestly scandals. But sex is a powerfully attractive goodness, more for its companionship than its
pleasure, and so this dynamic human experience is forever breaking
through, often in distorted forms, singly as every psychiatrist knows
and collectively as recent events have shown. R. Sipe records this fact
vividly in his book, *A Secret World*.[3]

So while the single state is an ideal for the few who voluntarily
choose it, the failure to grasp its complexity, the power of sex and the
companionship and pleasure it offers, and sexuality's essential link
with personality and connection with spirituality (to be described in

the chapter on marriage), all demand a rigorous re-examination of the subject.

Another source of the Church's flawed theology dates from the Middle Ages when natural law, particularly that of Aquinas, became supreme, reinforcing the idea that the principal purpose of sex was procreation. This concept has remained until the Second Vatican Council, which judged that procreation was still important (and who can disagree with that!) but that the other aims of intercourse were also important and were linked with love. In fact, as I shall show in the chapter on marriage, sexual intercourse is always in every act a life-giving force that occasionally gives new life. However, this deeply flawed tradition rests on the inability to see sexual pleasure as sacred, aided and abetted by the influence of Augustine, a genius but also a deeply wounded and scarred man. Reacting against his own problems and psychological ineptitude, he failed to understand sexual intercourse as one of the most powerful, loving and sacred energies of marriage.

It would not be true to say that the revolt, particularly by the young, against this tradition stems from a careful study on the above lines. Rather it follows from the emergence of detailed work in the nineteenth and twentieth centuries by people such as Freud, Kinsey, Masters and Johnson and others who popularised the subject. They drew attention to sexuality, liberated it from oppression and rehabilitated it as a vital human experience. The trouble with this sexual revolution is that, while it shed light on what was a dark world, its advances were in scientific understanding and the questions that dominated were those of technique, frequency and outlets of pleasure rather than the quality of the experience, love and personal meaning. In other words, the twentieth century liberated but also trivialised sex. The result has been that people, particularly the young, have reclaimed their bodies, from which they felt dispossessed, without appreciating the profound significance of sex, and the blame for this lies entirely with the Churches.

The Churches are rightly concerned about the trivialisation of sex, which has been called 'Liquid Love', sex as a disposable commodity.[4] But the answer is not a blanket command of 'Thou shalt not', which the young will rebel against as they feel misunderstood. In fairness to John Paul II, he has written a great deal about the body that is very illuminating, but the Church as a whole has not disseminated, clarified or stressed his insights.[5]

There is no alternative but for Christianity to take sexuality seriously. Theologians of all denominations need to explore the link between sex and love that was initiated at the Second Vatican Council and the meaning of adolescent sexuality, and to make the distinction between pre-conjugal and non pre-conjugal cohabitation which Adrian Thatcher, an Anglican theologian, has explored with great care.[6] Lay people need to be encouraged to study and proclaim the holiness of sexuality.

Sex can be the dynamite of disordered passion that Christianity has focused on or the grace of a sacred moment, linking Trinitarian and human relationships through love. What is certain is that, until Christianity recovers the truth about the subject, it will not regain the trust of society and develop a meaningful, serious voice to dialogue with the world.

Some critics make the naïve remark that the Church has no business to comment on and interfere with life in the bedroom. On the contrary, the Church has every right to be involved in this topic. However, this involvement must enhance the wonder of love in this sacred event, not negate it. The sacred has no boundaries and the bedroom is not an excluded zone from the life of love. Indeed it has a central role as yet not fully understood or appreciated by the core of Christianity. This failure is a powerful cause of the alienation of people from the Churches.

Chapter 7

The Spiritual Dimension

Having been graced to write this book in the seventy-fourth year of my life, as a cradle Catholic I have seen both the glory and the depths of the Church's liturgy. I make no attempt to cover this range in detail. Here I present some personal experiences, both positive and negative. I will cover prayer, Sacraments and the priesthood, starting with prayer, which we know is central to Christian life.

Prayer

From the Scriptures we know that Jesus prayed to his Father, so we can have no doubt about its central place of communication with God. We also know from Jesus that prayer is answered – if we ask, we will receive and this is reassuringly and extensively underlined. What are not extensively examined are the difficulties of prayer. Humanity needs concrete contact, a method of communication primarily through the senses. The doubting Thomas wanted to put his fingers in the wounds of Christ. When Jesus appeared again in the upper room and Thomas had the privilege of seeing and touching, his declaration of belief was greeted by Christ with the answer, 'Blessed are they who have not seen and yet believed' (John 20:29). This is a poignant moment in the Scriptures, for it summarises the perpetual problem we face in our desire for a concrete encounter with the unknown and invisible God to whom we pray.

There is no one who, from time to time, does not struggle with knowing whether or not their prayers are heard or answered. Spiritually, this is a well-recognised phenomenon, and the response from the pulpit is generally that God's ways are not ours, that his timetable is not our timetable, or that his answer comes in an unexpected form.

At the heart of prayer is blind faith, without knowing when, how and in what form the response will be. But there is no doubt that there is an inherent tendency to turn to God, frequently seen as, for example, at the death of Princess Diana, at times of suffering, need and celebration. My comment here would be that, although we should encourage prayer, there should also be a greater effort to unpack its difficulties.

Because people sometimes struggle to experience prayer's salutary and efficacious effect, I have developed a powerful distaste for the traditional situation in which someone goes to a priest for help with a difficult and complex problem. If at this point the priest has not got a clue how to handle the problem he may simply say, 'Pray and I will pray for you.' I do not doubt that prayer helps and a prayer will be said, but in these circumstances the answer can be a cop out. The person with the problem has probably already prayed and is still chained to his or her difficulty. Without doubting the spiritual validity of prayer, these situations require more. They need time to be spent, if necessary a long time, to listen to the story, not so much because an answer will be found, although it may be, but because the dialogue itself is God's presence in the encounter. The exchange is with the visible, listening God, the mystery and complexity of the situation is being unravelled without necessarily being solved, and the person is being heard, recognised and empathised with. These encounters are prayerful human answers. They come before any invisible answers arrive. These encounters are the prayer. 'I will say a prayer for you' is a form of cop out because the God in the 'I' does not respond to the 'you' in a way that gives human relief without necessarily being an answer to the problem.

In national and international disasters in which people gather to pray, we see not only a need to communicate with God and to seek his intervention, but above all, a need to give psychological vent to feelings, be they sorrow, anger or distress. 'In the beginning was the Word'(John 1:1), and the word is a powerful presence of God.

There still remain the millions who do not believe in, or who find it difficult to pray with, set prayers. Here we recognise the existence of prayer as we communicate with nature. In a beautiful sunset, the intensity of music, or indeed in any situation we can and do encounter God by appreciating the awe and wonder of the moment. We have been so keen to fix prayer within the four walls of the church that we forget God is everywhere and, above all, inside us. By emphasising mysticism and contemplation, both difficult and rare, we have ignored the awareness of God in the moment to moment of love that is one of the most powerful experiences of prayer.

In the course of my spiritual life, it is not the quantity of prayer that has expanded my sense of God but the range, the quality and finally the awareness that at every moment of my life, I am present in the immanence of God, particularly in and through love. My childhood practice of saying familiar set prayers has been supplemented by my continuous awareness of God outside these limits. As with many things in my life, I have broken through the limits, legal framework and fixed prayerful settings to an experience of the familiar phrase, 'Where love is, God is.'

Prayer is at the heart of every religious life but, because it is so extensive and difficult, we have tried to contain it in set moments and formulae, giving us the childish comfort that we have 'said' our prayers. Saying our prayers is undoubtedly an authentic moment. However, the sense of God and dialogue with him, which is what most prayer is, is infinitely more important. Ultimately prayer is the round-the-clock living awareness of interpersonal love with the 'other'. This inner awareness is far more important than the pyramidal attempt to reach the 'other out there'.

The Sacraments

Our immanent encounter with the transcendental reaches its climax in the Eucharist. From the Last Supper to the Consecration at every Mass Catholicism reaches the peak of prayer. In my lifetime I have participated in the pre-Vatican II Mass with the priest having his back to the people, speaking in Latin and delivering sermons that largely stressed sin, particularly sexual sin, rules and regulations. All these constituents diluted the sacred presence of Jesus and converted the Mass to a legal framework of ritual obedience. Theologians spent a great deal of their time defining what part of the Mass had to be 'heard' in order to fulfil the legal obligation. One 'heard' Mass rather than participated in and celebrated the most sacred moment of our faith. As I mentioned earlier, not eating meat on Fridays, not using contraception and 'hearing' Mass were the obligatory and recognisable common criteria of Catholic identity.

It was this distortion that I and millions of others faithfully followed and, for many who have left the Church, its echoes have been the source of their alienation. We did not know it then but 'Mass' was a large-scale Pavlovian exercise of sitting, standing and kneeling. Despite this, the sacred penetrated, but as an encounter that did not survive. Then came the Second Vatican Council. In the liturgy of the Mass the altar was moved to the centre of the church, the priest faced the people, spoke in their language, and preached homilies with an emphasis on Scripture, emphasising the supreme importance of love and marginalising the law. We participated, received the Host in our hands and drank the Blood of Christ. Of course, not every Mass emphasised all these details but the centre of the Incarnation became accessible in a way hardly ever experienced before.

For the last thirteen years I have been privileged to participate in Masses celebrated by a genuine post-Vatican II priest, who has given me an insight into the sacred event in which I am participating. Every moment of the Mass from the opening prayers, the Word of God, the homily and the Consecration to the final blessing are articulated with a solemnity and due respect for the sacredness of the moment. This experience makes me genuinely present in the mystery of the life, death and resurrection of the Son of God. I have also been present at Masses where the liturgy has been said, empty of the significance of the words, actions and moments. The Mass was celebrated in a hurry, prayers were gabbled without respect for the dignity they symbolised and the sacred was strangulated.

With words from the Old Testament and the New and through the meaning of the various sections, the Mass is something in which we participate fully, not only with due respect and attention but also by being theologically alive to its meaning. This requires an informed, theologically alive congregation of the people of God. Although we have made progress with theological formation, we are still far removed from an awareness that links us theologically with the sacred actions on the altar. We still often participate in sacred theatre. This is entirely due to the past and, up to a point, present emphasis on rules and the public collective consciousness that attendance at Mass is a duty rather than an opportunity to rejoice in the life, death and resurrection of Jesus Christ. There is a problem here for evangelisation. So many young people find Mass boring.

Despite my gripes, the Mass is a unique, wonderful Sacrament and the absence of millions from it is a very sad reality. The preceding chapters have focused on a number of factors that are alienating people of all ages. I will add one more here. John Paul II has issued an eloquent encyclical on the Eucharist, but with equal intensity has set his mind against married priests. The consequent shortage of priests has resulted in a Eucharistic famine all over the world. I am not saying that married priests will solve the current problems of withdrawal from the Church but this would help. There are numerous married ex-priests who could help in the present shortage. The acceptance of married Anglican priests makes the discipline of compulsory celibacy a real nonsense.

The other Sacrament I want to comment on is Reconciliation or Confession. Again, in pre-Vatican II days my memory was of queues waiting to go to Confession week after week. There is currently an almost total decline in individual Confession. Why? The answer is complex. First of all, a great deal of what was confessed involved Church-imposed discipline, responded to by an infantile, frightened population. Secondly, many of the sins confessed to were sexual in nature. Thirdly, the form of Confession did not encourage personal growth but depended on conditioned rituals, leading to frequent Confession that did not alter the personality but reinforced the infantilism. I have already stressed the need for the people of God to grow into emotional maturity and the importance of individual conscience and a growing awareness of the sacred significance of sexuality. Under these circumstances, individual Confession, not surprisingly, has declined.

What has not changed is the alienation from God in the lack of love that is always present within us, hence the full churches for services of Communal Reconciliation. But the present Curia, who are out of touch with the psychological and daily reality of the people of God, disapprove of this form of service and reiterate *ad nauseam* the importance of individual Confession. Nobody doubts there is a place for individual Confession, but it has to be acknowledged that its frequency in the past was the result of a flawed theology of Church rules and regulations, sexuality and the absence of growth. This inability to face the obvious truth is another reason for the alienation of the people of God. Many priests who do know their people continue with services of Communal Reconciliation with full churches and wait in almost empty churches for the time of individual Confession.

The Priesthood

Finally, at the centre of these and all other Sacraments stands the priest, a member of a diminishing and ageing group of men who in the past have been idealised by Catholics, hence the profound shock of the current sexual scandals. My experience of priests is divided between pre- and post-Vatican II days. Looking at them, without idealisation but with due respect, I now see that some of the pre-Vatican II priests were what I call sacramental technicians, pouring out ill-digested Thomistic theology and emphasising rules, sin and guilt. The vast majority were and are sincere men of God who serve in love and were and are exhausted by their pastoral work. Given the problems facing the Church in its institutional life and the compulsory and totally unnecessary rule of celibacy, it is not surprising that there are few vocations and those who come forward are often rigid, conservative personalities who are attracted by the current atmosphere in the official Church. A few still come forward because they truly identify with Christ's priesthood and many more will come forward, if and when things change, for the attraction of this holy state does not disappear. For this to happen patience is needed until the spirit of Vatican II returns and the core of its vision is realised.

Thankfully the majority of the people of God who still attend Mass and the other liturgies are not very preoccupied with Rome but, when appropriate, connect with their parish priest and bishop. To their credit, most bishops are not looking over their shoulders to Rome more than is necessary, and in private conversation are often appalled by what is happening in Rome. Instead of looking backwards, they look forward, are focused on Christ and so have the evangelisation of their people as a priority. The trouble for all of them is they are faced with so much bureaucracy that they are forced to spend much of their time with maintenance instead of mission.

Part Two

The Concept of Love

Chapter 8

The Centrality of Love

It is my conviction that Christianity's only answer to the challenges it faces within its own life and its message to the world must be in and through one word, 'love', interpreted with the specific needs of successive ages in mind. The message of love is very appropriate in our age, as its central concerns are relationships and their break-down. Although Christianity is saturated with statements about love, it falls profoundly short of actually living it out in the reality of re-lationships, and so poorly reflects the Trinity. The Judaeo-Christian tradition has been preoccupied with sin and with grace as the response. In all denominations, grace has been promoted principally through various liturgies, with the subtext of the Scriptures for the Reformers and, since Constantine, with law, rules and regulations in the Roman Catholic Church.

My obsession, and I use the word deliberately, is love and I shall use psychology to express love as a living reality. In support of my preoccupation, I shall use relevant scriptural passages, relying on Paul's conviction that love is the 'law of Christ' (Gal. 6:2) and, above all, on St John's text, 'God is love' (1 John 4:8). This chapter looks at the texts I will expand on, but is by no means a theological enterprise, since I am not a theologian and, from what I see of exegesis, there are many and various biblical interpretations. What follows is a layman's spiritual conviction.

Love is not an attitude but a way of life to be lived from moment to moment. There are two passages in the Old Testament that refer specifically to our love for God and our neighbour:

Listen, Israel: Yahweh our God is the one, the only Yahweh. You must love Yahweh your God with all your heart, with all your soul, with all your strength. Let these words I enjoin on you today stay in your hearts. (Deut. 6:4–5)

And from Leviticus,

You will not exact vengeance on, or bear any sort of grudge against, the members of your race but will love your neighbour as yourself. I am Yahweh. (Lev. 19:18)

In the New Testament, Jesus formulates the unique 'double commandment':

But when the Pharisees heard that he had silenced the Sadducees, they got together and, to put him to the test, one of them put a further question, 'Master, which is the greatest commandment of the Law?' Jesus said to him, 'You must love the Lord your God with all your heart, with all your soul, and with all your mind. This is the greatest and the first command-ment. The second resembles it: You must love your neighbour as yourself. On these two commandments hang the whole Law and the Prophets too.' (Matt. 22:34–40)

This double commandment reappears in Mark:

One of the scribes who had listened to them debating appreci-ated that Jesus had given a good answer and put a further question to him, 'Which is the first of all the commandments?' Jesus replied, 'This is the first: Listen, Israel, the Lord our God is the one, the only Lord, and you must love the Lord your God with all your heart, with all your soul, with all your mind and with all your strength. The second is this: You must love your neighbour as yourself. There is no command greater than these.' The scribe said to him, 'Well spoken, Master; what you have said is true, that he is one and there is no other. To love him with all your heart, with all your understanding and strength, and to love your neighbour as yourself, this is far more important than any burnt offering or sacrifice.' Jesus, seeing how wisely he had spoken, said, 'You are not far from the king-dom of God.' And after that no one dared to question him any more. (Mark 12:28–34)

And also in Luke:

> And now a lawyer stood up and, to test him, asked, 'Master, what must I do to inherit eternal life?' He said to him, 'What is written in the Law? What is your reading of it?' He replied, 'You must love the Lord your God with all your heart, with all your soul and with all your strength and with all your mind, and your neighbour as yourself.' Jesus said to him, 'You have answered right, do this and life is yours.' (Luke 10:25–8)

It is interesting that here the teaching of the great commandments is followed by the parable of the Good Samaritan (Luke 10:29–37), a unique demonstration of the meaning of loving our neighbours that applies through all time.

Proceeding to Paul, love is mentioned in all his letters and exhortations to love are very prominent. For Paul, love is not just an abstract ideal or one quality among others that make up the Christian life. It is powerfully present and active in history as an expression of God's own power at work, redeeming mankind, calling them to obedience and enabling them to obey. He links faith, being active in love and the Spirit (Gal. 5:22). Paul is important because for him love is not an abstract entity. Apart from connecting us with God, the link of love with the Spirit shows in visible, practical deeds of love in the Christian community.

Because the main theme of this book is our age's preoccupation with relationships and the love Christianity has to offer as the appropriate response, I shall quote only one famous and familiar text of Paul on love, frequently used at weddings:

> Though I command languages both human and angelic – if I speak without love, I am no more that a gong booming or a cymbal clashing. And though I have the power of prophecy, to penetrate all mysteries and knowledge, and though I have all faith necessary to move mountains – if I am without love, I am nothing. Though I should give away to the poor all that I possess, and even give up my body to be burned – if I am without love, it will do me no good whatever. [And here he continues with the first Christian counselling on marriage and human relationships.]

Love is always patient and kind; love is never jealous; love is not boastful or conceited, it is never rude and never seeks its own advantage, it does not take offence or store up grievances. [What better answer to sulking?] Love does not rejoice at wrongdoing, but finds its joy in the truth. It is always ready to make allowances, to trust, to hope and to endure whatever comes . . . As it is, these three remain: faith, hope and love, the three of them; and the greatest of them is Love.' (1 Cor. 13:1–13)

To say that I am moved by this passage is not original, but to suggest that it should be compulsory study in marriage preparation courses would be innovative, as its practice would save many marriages.

Finally I turn to John. Of course John's Gospel is full of descriptions of love, but I want to finish with one of the Johannine Epistles, once again very familiar and very much loved. (It is the passage I would like to have read at my funeral, as a prelude to the encounter I hope for with God in Heaven.)

> My dear friends,
> let us love each other,
> since love is from God,
> and everyone who loves
>   is a child of God and knows God.
> Whoever fails to love does not know God,
> because God is love.
> This is the revelation
>   of God's love for us,
> that God sent his only Son into the world
> that we might have life through him.
> Love consists in this:
> It is not we who loved God,
> but God loved us and sent his Son
> to expiate our sins.
> My dear friends,
> if God loved us so much,
> we too should love one another.
> No one has ever seen God,
> but as long as we love one another
> God remains in us

and his love comes to perfection in us.
This is the proof that we remain in him
and he in us,
that he has given us a share in his Spirit . . .
We have recognised for ourselves,
and put our faith in,
    the love God has for us.
God is love,
and whoever remains in love
    remains in God . . .
In love there is no room for fear,
but perfect love drives out fear,
because fear implies punishment
and no one who is afraid
    has come to perfection in love.
Let us love, then,
because he first loved us.
Anyone who says 'I love God'
and hates his brother
is a liar,
since whoever does not love the brother whom he can see
cannot love God whom he has not seen. (1 John 4:7–20)

In this very personal book I can reveal that the phrase 'God is love' is the core and centre of my faith. For forty years I have tried, using psychology, to translate this reality into living love in personal relationships, as my Christian contribution in opposition to the world's concept of love as inconstant, disposable and transitional. For me, the challenge of Christian love is that it is often described in abstract, philosophical terms and in exhortations, and not lived out in the life experienced by ordinary people in real situations. In the next chapter I shall demonstrate how psychology can be used to convert the concept of love into a living reality in human relationships.

Chapter 9

The Psychology of Love

This chapter outlines my belief that psychology is essential to our understanding of love in human relationships. Christianity's coolness towards dynamic psychology, now gradually receding, has been one of its many errors in the nineteenth and twentieth centuries, and I believe that Freud and a group of his successors, especially the British theorists decribed as Object Relations psychologists, are vital for the translation of love as portrayed in the scriptures into human terms. I will begin this chapter with a brief outline of Freud's psychology and go on to examine the contribution of the Object Relations psychologists.

Freud

Freud was an atheist and believed that religion was an infantile projection. Human beings are born helpless and dependent and, for Freud, God is the projected requirement of humanity: he is needed simply to offer the substitute security of the human father and religion is a neurosis. Jung believed in God and so has been consistently preferred by Christians, but Freud in particular has revolutionised our understanding of human beings.

Freud worked in Vienna at the end of the nineteenth century with patients we now call neurotic. The word 'neurotic' has complex meanings. On the one hand, it is used to describe collectively such conditions as anxiety, phobias, obsessive behaviour, hysteria and psychosomatic illness, and, on the other, personality disorders that express themselves in personal relationships. Very often the two categories are present simultaneously. In Freud's era, neuroses were as common as they are now. The therapies of the time advised going on holiday, a rest in the mountains, trips to the sea, baths and the use of sedatives. Freud found these and the use of hypnosis unsatisfactory and initiated 'talking therapy'. He invited the patient to lie on a couch, while he sat behind them, and encouraged the patient to talk freely about any subject that concerned them. He called this 'free association'. Freud did not intervene or give advice and was non-judgemental. In the course of the session, an allocated 50 minutes, Freud observed that the patient began to treat him as if he was a parental figure and to relive through him key early childhood experiences. Freud called this 'transference', a process that gave access to the earliest years of life, and particularly to forgotten memories. These memories could be of any kind but Freud noticed that they were frequently of a sexual and aggressive nature. Slowly he began to put together a theory about the human personality that revolutionised our understanding. He postulated that the human personality emerges from the presence and interaction of two instincts, sexuality and aggression, and their vicissitudes in the course of the personality's development.

Freud was a good writer and he left a large body of work explaining his theories. Beginning with his theory about these two key instincts, he built a schema of the personality containing three elements, the id, the ego and the superego. He postulated that there was an unconscious pool of the instincts situated in the id, urging the satisfaction of the pleasure principle, which was held in check by an equally unconscious presence in the superego, where the parental and other prohibitions resided. Thus the superego kept the drives in check. A tension was created between the id and the superego, the two unconscious worlds of the psyche, mediated through the ego, which was the conscious source of vigilance, working on the reality principle and promoting what was considered safe and acceptable.

Freud postulated that sexual and aggressive traumas, particularly the former, which were hidden in the unconscious exerted an influence by generating anxiety which, in his opinion, was then transformed into neurotic symptoms including fears, obsessions, hysterical manifestations, depressions, and especially suppressed anger. In the course of analysis, the talking therapy was intended to render the unconscious traumas conscious and help the patient to identify them and own them. The theory was that if the source of the stress was removed, the symptoms would disappear. It did not always work, then or now! Freud, however, was not primarily concerned with therapeutic results but was fascinated with the schema he proposed for the foundation of the personality, particularly the presence of instincts or drives, the existence of the unconscious and the presence of dreams which revealed what was hidden in the unconscious.

He also theorised that in the first year of life the energy of the libido and aggression are situated in the mouth, which is lined with mucous membrane, a smooth lining that gives sensuous pleasure. This he called the oral phase. In the second and third year this was replaced by a phase at the other end of the gastro-intestinal tract, and in the fifth year he reached the well-known triangular situation when a boy seeks sexual fusion with his mother, is barred by the fear of his father and castration and withdraws from his desire for his mother, now identifying with his father. This so-called resolution of the Oedipus complex is central to Freudian theory. The Electra complex is the female equivalent.

Freud also suggested that there are mechanisms for removing material from consciousness. A defence is a psychological mechanism which diverts the anxiety created from emotional trauma from the conscious to the unconscious, and most of these defences are themselves unconscious. He identified the following common defence mechanisms:

- **Repression**, a process in which the anxiety engendered from emotional trauma is transferred into the unconscious. While there, it has an enduring energy of its own that continues to cause stress and agitation. This unconscious mechanism can be compared with suppression, which is a deliberate process of putting something out of one's mind, and a favourite of a previous generation of moral theologians, who regarded it as removing a temptation from one's mind.
- **Denial**, an unconscious disclaimer of an unacceptable, disagreeable happening. This is very often used as a way of denying responsibility when people do not want to face a present stress. The distinction between unconscious denial and a deliberate conscious avoidance is at the heart of many disputes, and can

escalate into accusing another person of lying, cheating or being deliberately nasty. This can play havoc in marriage.

- **Projection**, a defence mechanism which involves attributing one's own peculiarities, feelings and beliefs to others and, in so-called projective identification, receiving them back as if they belong to others. Projection is a very common mechanism in which we see in others what we do not want to, or cannot, see in ourselves, believing, for example, that others and not ourselves are angry or jealous, and this can prove destructive in intimate relationships such as marriage.

- **Identification**, the opposite of projection, in which we adopt the qualities of others and accept them as the product of our own efforts.

- **Substitution** or **conversion**. As these names imply, this allows us to channel our anxieties and tensions into, for example, physical symptoms such as headaches, pains or other forms of disability. In this context, hysteria is the process whereby emotional stress is converted into a physical or psychological symptom. Freud began his studies with a classic case of hysteria.

- **Reaction formation**, which involves the development of a quality or trait opposing some strong unconscious drive or conflict, for example, the extreme puritan reacting against strong sexual urges, or an extreme cleanliness reacting against a fear of dirt. Reaction formation defences are frequently found in Christians who oppose sex and are unable to see or tolerate its goodness.

- **Rationalisation**. This is one of the commonest defences and takes the form of a rational explanation which is used in conjunction with denial to avoid an unpleasant situation. Ultimately rationalisation is used in order to conceal our own real motives, and so to avoid accepting, doing, or believing something. For example, a dissatisfied husband will work late because he does not want to go home, a partner who dislikes sex will produce a physical complaint such as a headache, and an alcoholic will find a reason to be near a source of liquor.

- **Sublimation**. This uses the energy of our instincts by channelling it in constructive paths towards the higher realms of religion, art, literature and the wide range of socially and spiritually acceptable good works.

- **Regression**, a mechanism which returns our needs, outlook and attitudes to those of an earlier emotional age. Regression is very common as, for example, when we are in physical or emotional pain, we want to be treated like a child, picked up, comforted, hugged and sympathised with.

So how much of orthodox Freudian theory has stood the test of time? Orthodox psychoanalysis as an effective therapeutic tool is used less and less. On the other hand, in the modified forms of psychotherapy and counselling it is used extensively. Here the elements of articulating stress, being listened to, slowly discerning dysfunctional patterns of relationships, reducing anxiety, growing in self-esteem and assertion, reducing anger and growing in the capacity to love are changes of profound importance, even if the means of change are very different from Freud's original theories. Freud's theory of the unconscious and its defences has endured the test of time, and has become part and parcel of everyday life. It has extended immeasurably the range of human freedom and moral life and has brought healing within the reach of everyone. Our understanding of defence mechanisms and the process of transference and counter-transference is transforming human relationships and the range and possibility of love.

Object Relations Psychology

Object Relations psychology is not well known even within psychological circles, and hardly at all outside them, with the possible exception of Bowlby. One of its difficulties, and indeed a universal one with all dynamic psychology, is the language it uses.

All Object Relations psychologists, apart from Bowlby and Fairbairn, are successors of Freud and use his theories, but with one great difference. For Freud, the personality emerged from the gradual internal vicissitudes of the two instincts, sexuality and aggression, solely within the child. The Object Relations theorists insisted that this is a wrong view – while not denying the presence of the instincts, they took the view that the personality is shaped by the interaction between the instincts and the parents. Thus the loving capacity of the parents was crucial for the growth of the personality and the ultimate development of a loving adult.

The current and perennial significance of the nurture versus nature debate is intimately connected with Object Relations psychology. The importance of parents has been understood for a long time but our understanding of how they facilitate and shape growth owes much to these theories. Since this book is not primarily a textbook of psychology I will confine myself to examining the ideas of four well-known theorists, Melanie Klein, Winnicott, Fairbairn and Bowlby. (A useful book is *An Introduction to Object Relations* by Lavinia Gomez.[1])

Melanie Klein

Melanie Klein has been very influential to this day. For her, the ego, the sense of a separate existence, is there from the very start of life, unlike Freud who saw the start of life as non-differentiated and gradually taking cohesive shape. She believed that the body was pivotal, not for its physiological drives but for its hopes, fears and wishes.

She saw that central to life was the tension between love and the urge to destroy, occurring in an interaction between the inner self and the outer world. In this interaction she described two basic positions that cope with her central concerns, the experience and management of anxiety. She attached great importance to anxiety, postulating that at birth the child's inner world is chaotic with anxieties and fears. She believed that the baby deals with these in three ways:

1. by experiencing food, sucking at the breast or bottle. This is a good and loving experience.
2. by separating or 'splitting' good experiences and bad experiences.
3. by projecting bad experiences and feelings outside itself, usually onto its mother.

Splitting and projecting are two basic mechanisms of survival. Klein described this as a paranoid-schizoid position. Nearly all adults use similar mechanisms. In order to survive, we split our experiences into the good and the bad, identify with the good which we retain, and get rid of the bad and push it outside ourselves through projection onto other people or areas, from personal relationships right through to politics. The cry of 'It's not my fault, but somebody else's' is a universal psychological mechanism. The essence of psychological maturity is when we cease to project, accept responsibility for our actions, stop blaming others and learn to love them.

I want also to draw attention to the good feelings that Klein attaches to food and to remember that Jesus was also keen on food: dining with friends; the multiplication of the loaves and fishes as an act of compassionate love; and finally his giving of himself through his body and blood and its recurrent availability in the Eucharist.

In the next three months of the baby's life, which Klein called the depressive phase, the baby expresses its anxieties through angry frustration, due to its dissatisfaction with what it now feels is an empty breast. It now screams, bites and attacks the 'object', here understood as the breast which represents the whole person of the mother. The experience of aggressively chewing the breast produces conflict. The 'object', i.e. the mother, is now an object of both love and frustration, giving rise to ambivalence, distress, sadness and guilt. But Klein offers hope. Without realising this, she brings together faith, hope and love. The baby realises that being angry, hurt, sad and feeling guilty carry the possibility of reparation. Tantrums and the accompanying anger give rise to guilt, the sense of the loss of the mother's love, and the need to regain her love through reparation and forgiveness. Klein postulated that anger, hurt, guilt, pain, a sense of loss of love and the urge for reparation, forgiveness and reconciliation is a basic psychological mechanism acquired during the first six months of life.

If readers find this timetable difficult to accept, they have my sympathy. What is not open to dispute is that this cycle is universal at all ages, and is central to love and to Christianity's core belief in sin and forgiveness. We can speculate further on its closeness to the spiritual cycle of original sin, Christ's death, reparation, forgiveness and reconciliation with mankind.

To summarise, Klein packs into the first six months of life what she observed and interpreted as a child analyst with toddlers. Her complex psychology is based on the presence of anxiety in the baby that is comforted by food, milk from breast or bottle, and an ability to separate its inner world into good experiences which it retains and bad experiences which it projects outside itself and onto its mother.

The 'bad' is its anxiety and anger which can damage the mother – this damage leads to hurt, pain, guilt, loss of the mother's love and depression, but can also produce a longing for reparation and forgiveness. Faith in life is possible through the goodness of the mother, and hope through the desire for reconciliation. Whatever the timetable, these cycles are apparent from childhood to the grave.

Donald Winnicott

For Winnicott, a paediatrician turned analyst, there was no such thing as a baby on its own but always a dyad, the baby and an adult, usually the mother. The baby-mother encounter fosters the unique importance of love of closeness and togetherness. Like Freud, he believed that although the baby has drives, it is not a seething bundle of need-seeking gratification, and like Klein, he postulated that the baby is constantly on the edge of anxiety. The mother is someone who recognises this anxiety, primarily expressed through crying, and identifies with it. Winnicott was constantly faced with the task of reassuring mothers about their handling of their babies, and he did this by coining the phrase 'the "good enough" mother'.

The 'good enough' mother physically holds the baby and provides security against the terror of disintegration, of falling or of being dropped. The baby is further satisfied, i.e. loved, by being fed at the right times and by having its nappy changed, which makes the baby feel clean. For Winnicott, the mother expresses her love by responding to the child's physical needs through holding and touch. He recognised the unique importance of touch for love, something that Christianity needs to learn, given its longstanding anxieties about physical touch and its connection with sex. Winnicott also recognised that the mother helped to bring the outside world close to the child in a safe way through feeding and toys. Thus he stressed love in terms of holding, handling and closeness to the outside world, all of which make the child feel safe and secure, which is central to love.

The concept of the 'good enough' mother is very important to Christianity, which is crucially aware of sin and our repeated and often unsuccessful efforts to overcome it, and to love wholeheartedly. The 'good enough' mother represents our 'good enough' efforts to persevere in overcoming our failures and limitations. Finally,

Winnicott described the so-called 'transitional object', well known in the *Peanuts* cartoons. He knew, as we all do, that the baby has gradually to separate itself from its mother, which is profoundly anxiety-provoking. The child tries to overcome this anxiety by holding on to a favourite cuddly toy, a piece of rag or a blanket which represents the mother, a transitional object which gives a feeling of safety and comfort. Some religiously orientated psychologists have described religion as a transitional object between ourselves and God, which we gradually take in or internalise to make God safe inside us.

Winnicott continued to stress the importance of the mother, who gives a sense of togetherness by her proximity, security by holding, trust and reliability by her availability for feeding and cleaning, and predictability and safety in the process of separation. Who can deny that in all this we see the experience of adult love, and that the opposite of these characteristics is felt as rejection?

Ronald Fairbairn

Fairbairn suggested that the ego or 'I' is present at birth, at the beginning, and that the libido was the energy not, as Freud postulated, the source of the personality. Unlike Freud, Fairbairn contended that the personality is primarily not pleasure-seeking but object-seeking. In other words, our deepest need is for contact with others and our most basic anxiety is therefore separation anxiety.

At birth we are whole, undivided and driven to relate to our mothers, and one of the basic concerns in life is the baby's doubt whether the mother loves it for itself, or accepts the baby's love. Here is a profound explanation for the difficulties some people have in giving and receiving love, and this trauma appears to be universal and fundamental, in that no one feels certain of being loved and valued for who they are. In marriage the two commonest complaints are: 'You don't love me – you only want me for my body', and, 'You don't love me – you only want me for my money.' These universal problems do not only apply in marriage: in any close relationship there is always the fear of being used or exploited, and not loved.

Thus for Fairbairn, the basic necessity from childhood onwards is love and, since even the most perfect parents cannot give perfect love in the right amount and form, even a minimum amount of dissatisfaction with love received is a universal trauma. How do we deal with this trauma? First, he suggested that we separate this pain, render it unconscious and place it inside us as a damage limitation exercise. We continue to relate to others with this split-off need. His psychological explanation of how we deal with this splitting-off is complex, but here is a simple summary:

1. We can live with the certainty that we will never be loved, like someone waiting by the telephone for a call that they are certain will never come.
2. We can persuade ourselves that we do not need love and can do without it. At the extreme end of this trauma, which Fairbairn calls the schizoid state, we feel empty, dead or futile.

The internal feeling of lack of love and of being unlovable is linked with an equivalent amount of unconscious anger. So when we try to love a person who is hungry for love, instead of being thanked or appreciated, we may be surprised by an outburst of anger.

This central issue of the universal need for love from others and an equally universal disappointment may, of course, be described as the human condition of original sin, but it is vital to recognise its psychological roots and not to pretend that love and its deprivation are not central. Christianity can be guilty of fobbing off psychological wounds with the legitimate but insufficiently satisfactory answers of prayer, Scripture and the Sacraments. Fairbairn's is one of the most powerful psychological understandings of the scriptural case for love which I presented in the previous chapter. For Fairbairn our primary trauma is the split within ourselves because of insufficient love. We seek it for the whole of our lives and life's drama is where, how, in what form and how successfully we find it.

John Bowlby

I had the privilege of hearing John Bowlby lecture shortly before his death in 1994. He took a profoundly different theoretical position from other Object Relations psychologists on the human personality. Unlike Freud and his successors, he was not satisfied that satiation of hunger, infantile sexuality and physical handling were sufficient for understanding love and human bonds. Rather than examining instincts, he outlined a very powerful theory of affective attachment, based on the human ability to make affectionate bonds. This was based in turn on the science of ethology (the study of how animals form bonds with their parents). He suggested that human bonds of affection are similarly dependent on vision, sound, touch and smell. These parameters allow us to form bonds of affection with our parents and research suggests that such bonds apply from the cradle to the grave.

This parental bond makes us feel safe and is the basis of our emotional security. In this theory the problem is separation, which gives rise to anxiety, anger and depression. The baby cannot stand this separation for too long and recalls the mother by crying. As a toddler he will take a few steps away from her, always looking back to her for security, especially if a stranger is present. For Bowlby this bond of affection is the basis of love-giving by parents through continuous and constant loving support. This security or love is absent when:

- One or both parents are positively unresponsive to the child's care-eliciting behaviour, experienced as continuous rejection.
- Persistent threats not to love the child are used as a punishment or means of control.
- One or both parents threaten to abandon the family or to commit suicide.
- The mother threatens to abandon the child.
- The child is made to feel guilty by being blamed for parental illness or death.

These factors are described by Bowlby as contributing to poor psychological parenting, leading to an insecure person, constantly afraid to rely on himself and terrified of separation or the threat of being left. These people live constantly with the fear of being abandoned and perpetually seek reassurance that they are loved.

Bowlby believed that affectional bonds give rise to a basic security which allows us to live alone, not in fear and capable of loving and receiving love. This theory explains bereavement with its sequence of painful loss, anxiety, depression and gradual recovery as we internalise the lost loved one, in the way that we internalise our mother's love to give us security.

It is now widely recognised from the work of the four psychologists I have mentioned that the way that parental care is given contributes fundamentally to the mental health of the individual and to their capacity to feel secure and to be a loving person. For this reason dynamic psychology is vital to Christianity and later I will suggest that it should be one of the handmaids of theology alongside philosophy.

Chapter 10

Intimate Relationships in Childhood and Adulthood

Psychological growth in Western culture follows a simple line. We start life in a sense of fused oneness with our mothers. The pattern of our life is a process of gradual physical, emotional and cognitive separation, a key point coming at the age of four or five when we begin school. Another key point of development is at about the age of twelve, when puberty arrives with its significant incest taboo, compelling us to look outward and away from our parents for sexual and emotional relationships. This continues to develop during adolescence until, ultimately, we form a second intimate relationship, usually expressed nowadays firstly in cohabitation, and then in marriage.

During the interval of separation between the first and second intimate relationships, emotional patterns are laid down governing our capacity to love. These patterns come into operation after puberty, initially in transitional relationships, and become permanently established in our second intimate relationships. I use the word 'pattern' because some people are concerned about the impact that one or two isolated incidents in their childhood will have on them. Although a solitary adverse event may have consequences in adult life, it is more usual that positive and negative patterns laid down over time become deeply rooted and influence subsequent adult relationships.

One of the most frequent questions I am asked is whether, according to this dynamic psychological model, there is any hope for those who had damaging experiences in their first intimate experience in childhood. It is true that we often see emotional damage in childhood having consequences, but I do not believe that there is an inevitable emotional determinism. Although some consequences remain, people have amazing capacities to overcome their difficulties, either by themselves or, more often, by marrying or linking themselves to another person who heals them by offering second chances.

Looking again at emotional patterns in which security and the ability to give and receive love are established, research clearly shows that irritability, moodiness, and angry outbursts in childhood are followed by the repetition of these traits, associated with juvenile delinquency and crime, later on. One theoretical pattern of the personality already referred to, that of John Bowlby's affective formation of bonds, has been widely studied and I shall use it to illustrate the child-adult continuity of the personality. The baby forms an emotional attachment with its mother, which is the basis of love. This is formed by recognising her face and the sound of her voice, and touch through holding and being held. This attachment gives the baby comfort and affection. The mother or other substitutes act as a secure base to which the child returns under stress. 'Attachment behaviour' is held to characterise human beings from cradle to grave.

Further research by Ainsworth and her colleagues has shown that three types of attachment in children continue into adult life. The first type of attachment is called 'secure' attachment, in which the child or adult perceives the caretaker as reliable and trustworthy. The largest group, comprising about 60 per cent of people, display this type of attachment. A further 20 per cent of people can be described as 'anxious resistant'. Children in this group interpose contact with angry resistant behaviour. The remaining 20 per cent are described as 'avoidant', and these children actively avoid contact with the caretaker and are distressed. Anxious, ambivalent and avoidant people have difficulties in trusting others and have a marked fear of being abandoned.[1]

These discoveries are of paramount importance. They help us to understand what sort of person we are, with the secure variety feeling loved and accepted and the anxious and avoidant struggling with these issues. In the world of relationships, the 'other' is considered from the view of how they are likely to respond to us. This model guides our expectations of whether we can trust others, and whether we feel acceptable and loveable ourselves.

Work with six-year-old children shows that those with secure attachments have positive, self-accepting images. At an older stage, there is a link between secure attachment and confident, accepting people with the capacity to get close to and trust others. On the other hand, anxious, ambivalent people desire to merge (to get as close as possible and to cling), fearing that they will not be loved and needing constant reassurance. Avoidant individuals report the lowest capacity to trust and the most cynical beliefs about love.

Bowlby and his successors have given us some of the most important findings about the links between love and relationships. Up to a point, the ability to trust and love is determined from infancy, with the continuity of patterning from childhood to adulthood having particular consequences for marriage. Object Relations psychological theories from Fairbairn to Bowlby show us how love fares from childhood to adulthood, developing in these childhood years within what I have called the first intimate relationship. Needless to say, the quality of the environment parents provide facilitates or acts against the growth of love, with genetics contributing.

So far I have concentrated on the emotional patterns of relationships. I want now to look at cognitive patterns. These are equally important and concern everyday exchanges of justice, fairness, responsibility, reciprocity and rules. Piaget[2] researched this aspect of children's development by watching them play with marbles and offering scenarios that require making judgements. Kohlberg[3] followed Piaget and, in the findings of both, it appears we move on an ascending scale of maturity through the following stages:

1. having no concept of rules
2. blind obedience to rules
3. evaluation of rules depending on circumstances
4. autonomy from rules
5. altruism.

Finally, in Christian terms, we arrive at the absolute principal of unconditional love, which we see throughout the history of Christianity, in the sacrifice of martyrs. On a more sombre note, at present we are witnessing suicide bombers dying for their cause.

As far as the Roman Catholic Church is concerned, the maturity of its organisation and life depends on the stage of psychologically cognitive development it has reached. I believe that from the time of Constantine, the balance of the Church's life has been tilted in favour of rules and law and against love. A fundamental turning towards rules and law and away from reflecting the life of love of Jesus as its centre was taken at this point in history. I am well aware that, in an institution like the Church, law and rules are needed, but excessive emphasis on the latter is dangerous, as it can lead to an undue exercise of power. As individuals, we have to operate on the basis of living by rules which have been thoroughly evaluated and act freely as conscience dictates. This level of maturity does not sit comfortably with the atmosphere that prevails in the Church today, and consequently we live in a Church whose level of maturity is sharply contrasted with Jesus' ultimate command to love.

Most people, of course, do not live by Jesus' double commandment of unconditional love for God and for others. They operate by reciprocal love. The amount of love I give depends on the amount of love I receive, the number of favours I do for others depends on the number they do for me and so on. Our present age also emphasises the absolute importance of the self and the present at the expense of the other and the future: of disposable relationships at the expense of enduring love. Although Christianity condemns this outlook, I believe that it fails to provide mature alternatives for love, marriage and sexuality because we have no persuasive models of love to offer. In all these areas our best and repeated offer that both young people within the church and the world outside hear frequently are the words 'Don't' and 'Thou shalt not'. My book will explore how the Church can begin to offer the word 'Do'.

Dynamic psychology and human wisdom assert that our second intimate relationships, lived out in the sustained intimacy of marriage and friendship, have a tendency to repeat the positive and negative learned patterns of love of our first relationship. This is the psychological basis of my methodology of love within marriage and friendship that brings, in contemporary terms, the baggage of the past of childhood into current relationships. As far as marriage is concerned, its survival depends on whether the past each spouse brings is on balance more positive than negative, and how the two pasts interact.

In the contemporary world there has been a major shift in the measure of the success of intimate relationships, particularly marriage, from the fulfilment of established roles to the quality of the relationship. By and large, neither society nor Christianity have quite adapted to this shift which requires a completely new strategy of education, preparation for and sustaining of relationships, dependent on love.

Chapter 11

Marriage: a Loving Community

The Second Vatican Council, against fierce conservative opposition from the Curia, initiated some dramatic changes in the Church's understanding of marriage. For centuries marriage was described in terms of primary ends, the procreation and upbringing of children, and secondary ends, mutual help and the relief of concupiscence. In the 1930s, 1940s and 1950s there was a great deal of opposition to this arid description, including my own. In my first book on marriage, I described it as:

> ... a God-given lifelong loving community, created to ensure the most appropriate conditions for the promotion of life, the life of the children and that of the spouses. [Marriage] is based on a series of relationships of love that in chronological order are those of the spouses, the spouses and their children, and the children among themselves. It is upon the physical, psychological and social integrity of these relationships, participating in the sacramental life of grace, that the essence of marriage ultimately rests.[1]

The book was published in 1967 and the cover declared that it was the fruit of 15 years of deliberation on marriage and sex. This date suggests that I have been preoccupied with this subject for over 50 years. This quotation formed the basis of my innumerable further studies on the subject, and was the first example of one of my views being validated as a definition of marriage by the Second Vatican Council.

While my current theology on marriage is widely accepted and taught, my views on sexuality, although in keeping with those of

Vatican II, are not equally welcome because of my non-acceptance of the teaching of *Humanae Vitae*, which is now largely rejected by the overwhelming majority of Catholics. Indeed, the young are hardly aware of this teaching, but it remains the official policy of the Magisterium. My conservative critics, few as they are, find it difficult to accept that I lecture as a Roman Catholic all over the world. Nevertheless my conviction that love should form the basis of sexuality is very much in keeping with views of the Council.

The Council stressed marriage and the family as a community of life and love.[2] This emphasis on love was a notable feature of the Council's teaching and had a profound impact. As I have said before, however welcome the word 'love', there is a profound difference between its abstract and concrete manifestations. Christianity is saturated with an awareness of the concept of love, but falls very short in making it a reality.

John Paul II is very keen on the concept of love but that this is abstract love is shown clearly in his encyclical *Familiaris Consortio*, an exhortation on marriage and the family which is based very much on conciliar teaching on the subject. He says:

> God created man in his own image and likeness, calling him to existence, through love, he called him at the same time for love . . . Love is therefore the fundamental and innate vocation of every human being . . . Sexuality . . . is realised in a truly human way only if it is an integral of the love by which a man and woman commit themselves totally to one another until death . . . The Spirit which the Lord pours forth gives a new heart and renders man and woman capable of loving one another as Christ loved us . . . The content of participation in Christ's life is also specific conjugal love involving a totality in which all the elements of the person enter – appeal to the body and instinct, power of feeling and affectivity, aspiration of the spirit and of will . . . hence the family has the mission to guard, reveal and communicate love.

I could continue but I will end with a superb declaration,

> Man cannot live without love. He remains a being that is incomprehensible for himself, his life is senseless if love is not

revealed to him, if he does not encounter love, if he does not experience and make it his own, if he does not participate intimately in it.

Like many of his encyclicals, this is a masterpiece. I had the privilege of listening to him speak before he became Pope and I was mesmerised by his words on love. This magnificent oration on love is couched in philosophy and Christian ideals as so much of his theology is. But for the ordinary person, the person who is to live and make real this love, there is no concrete example of interpersonal love. There are no psychological examples, or, for that matter, examples of real loving experience. On the other hand, there are concrete negative comments about contraception, divorce and abortion. I wholeheartedly agree with him on these last two points, but as I have mentioned before, the danger for Christianity is that we are perceived as negative, emphasising the 'Don'ts', rather than the 'Dos', the positive, practical patterns of love. Prohibitions and rules abound, but what about loving practice?

The lack of association between abstract and concrete love in my quotations from the encyclical may be perceived as a criticism of John Paul II but it is not intended to be anything of the sort. It is an example of my much larger general complaint that our theology is too theoretical, too abstract and too analytical and not located in concrete human experience. A legitimate answer would be that the Pope lays down principles and invites lay people to make their own distinct contribution. This is part of my intention in writing this book, but my experience has been that previously when the laity have volunteered concrete contributions about contraception, i.e. that *Humanae Vitae* does not reflect the truth about sexual intercourse, not a scrap of official affirmative importance has been attached to these observations.

When the people of God, and indeed the bishops of Britain, suggested that the rule of excluding the remarried from receiving the Eucharist be relaxed, once again an inexcusable obdurate wall was met. The recent encyclical on the Eucharist is magnificent but it is accompanied by a rigid prohibition, the man-made law of priestly celibacy. A suggestion that love be linked to sexual ethics is met by the perpetuation of the most unchristian sexual morality, for example the recent statement on homosexuality. There is a yawning gap between the theory and words of love and practice. In the area of marriage and sexuality, love needs to be connected with living reality. I recognise that my critics may repeat that encyclicals and papal pronouncements are there to offer principles and that it is for the laity, in the case of marriage, to translate them into action. I believe this is not satisfactory. I would like to reaffirm that my arguments are not intended as attacks on the Pope himself, but as a defence of the principle of informing lay people.

For example, I believe the encyclical on the theology of marriage should have used contributions from married people to illustrate in broad terms how to translate this love into everyday life. Other experts have been consulted in other encyclicals, but on the subject of marriage, which has one of the most intimate links with the life of the Church, the excellent but theoretical approach of John Paul II means that the connection with real life has been lost. Much theology is deficient in this respect – it can seem to provide golden rules, but can end up being empty to the ordinary person. This is caused by theologians living parallel lives to the laity, but rarely meeting lay people. There is a real danger that theologians end up writing for each other, particularly on the topics of marriage, sex and love which are crucial for lay people. The prohibitions on contraception, sterilisation and abortion are all uttered repeatedly and not balanced by the concrete goodness of living love. The theology of the Incarnation is much more than philosophy, and while it deserves abstract consideration, it also needs practical commentaries on human life that should reflect both positive and negative issues.

The distinction between the abstract and the concrete can be seen more fully in John Paul II's commentaries on marriage, sexuality and love in his series of weekly audiences between 1979 and 1981. I have read these in full in *The Theology of the Body*[3] and in abbreviated form with a commentary in *Feast of Love*.[4] In case my conservative critics feel that I am obsessed with my ambivalence to his being a brilliant academic and at the same time disconnected and alienated from living love, particularly through his theological style, let me quote from Mary Durkin, a devotee and interpreter of John Paul, in *Feast of Love*,

Unfortunately, the Pope uses an obscure theological style which causes most people including theologians, bishops, priests and pastoral workers problems of understanding.[5]

In his remarks, he stresses original solitude, original unity, original nakedness and the nuptial meaning of the body. These are all profound observations and the Pope should be congratulated on entering this minefield of the body for the Church. I repeat however, there is a profound difference between this abstract theology and concrete living in love.

Part Three

Marriage and the Family

Chapter 12

Falling in Love and Loving

Having nailed my colours to the mast of living love, I now turn to marriage and the family.[1] In this section I intend to expand on and develop Vatican II's concept of marriage as 'a community of love and life'.

Falling in Love

During the stage of the psychological life cycle which comes after puberty and adolescence, there are a variety of frequent and transitory stages of falling in love that I will consider in detail. Research has shown that the commonest draw towards being in love comes from the realisation that the lover provides something that one needs. The most usual need is deliverance from isolation and aloneness, the seeking of another person who, Fairbairn suggests, is our principal universal need. Research also indicates that we are more likely to fall in love with someone when some or all of the following background features are present:

- **Similarity:** the person has similar attitudes and personality traits to our own.
- **Propinquity:** the person is familiar, lives near to us and is someone we spend time with and spend time thinking about.
- **Desirable characteristics** in the other person, especially their appearance.
- **Reciprocal liking**, that is being liked by each other, both in general terms and as expressed through self-disclosure.

- **Social influences:** the person is someone who our family and friends like and approve of.
- **Need fulfilment:** the person fulfils our need in some way, for example by having a stable personality.

These factors can bring us together, but there are additional features more specific to falling in love, such as:

- **Physical arousal:** palpitations, sweating and excitement, especially in chance encounters. We may enter a room and see someone whose appearance, voice, eyes and posture release the strong physiological features mentioned above, giving the feeling of falling in love at first sight.
- **A readiness to enter into a relationship.** This may depend on the stage we are at in our life cycle. For example, if we have low self-esteem, we may be more open to a relationship that makes us feel wanted.
- **Exclusiveness:** the desire to be alone with the beloved.
- **Mystery**. This is hard to define but is readily felt and seen as a trait in the other person.

There are two major paths to falling in love, the sudden experience and the slow convergence after appropriate affiliation. Falling in love can also be explained in terms of Bowlby's attachment theory. As we have already seen, this theory states that we form strong bonds of affective attachment through sight (appearance), sound (the voice) touch (physical contact) and smell (the perfume industry!).

Whatever the characteristics of falling in love, it is a universal experience within Western society and has certain powerful, widely recognised features. In this state people feel totally preoccupied with the beloved. The beloved is idealised in the sense that they are seen as possessing the most beautiful body, mind and heart. Despite what others, including their family and friends, think, people in love are utterly convinced that their beloved is almost perfect. Their good points are exaggerated and their bad points glossed over. They are easily forgiven because the whole purpose of the relationship is to spend the maximum time together in loving harmony. Whatever the doubts in others' minds, there are none in those who have fallen in love.

This state has been variously described as limerance or mania, and includes the features of physical and emotional excitement listed above, together with the presence of total preoccupation. The experience of falling in love can be relentlessly pursued by extroverts who seek excitement, and can result in infidelity, repeated divorce and remarriage for those who constantly hunger to repeat the experience. It also explains the appeal of romantic fiction and films and the desire for happy endings, because these echo the ecstasy and the yearning of falling in love.

Loving

Falling in love is often a prelude to cohabitation, and ultimately for most people, to marriage. Marriages nowadays may last for fifty years or more. Although there are frequent descriptions of passionate and companionate love, the latter describing love in modern marriage, to the best of my knowledge there is no detailed and comprehensive book about love experienced day by day over this long period of time. There is plenty of cynicism about long-term marriage, which is believed to induce feelings of boredom and a sense of being jailed for life, struggles with familiarity and the waning of sexual desire. These factors are repeatedly offered as the reasons for divorce, coupled with the perceived excitement of falling in love again, and a desire for freedom to try repeatedly for new intimate relationships and alternative romantic experiences. In other words, critics say that marriage can and does become a bore and we should all have the right and freedom to try again, and again if necessary. This is a widespread view that Christianity has failed to counter with an alternative and deeper understanding of love.

In actual fact, at a very minimum, between 40 and 60 per cent of married people stay together, and we need to ask what keeps them together. Here we come to Vatican II's definition of marriage as a community of love. I have persistently pleaded for the need in Christian theology for a living description of marriage, as this is one of the widest prevailing forms of loving, and affects the emotional fulfilment of the majority of men and women. When Klinger posed the question, 'What is it that makes life meaningful?'[2] almost all respondents mentioned being loved and wanted. In a national survey, Campbell and others found that most people consider it more important to have a happy family life and good friends than to have financial security.[3]

I have been describing marital love as 'loving' for nearly 30 years, in hundreds of lectures in Britain and overseas and in numerous books starting with *Marriage, Faith and Love* in 1981.[4] Although it has been pointed out that many ordinary experiences in everyday life such as playfulness and involvement with neighbours do not play a central part in my schema, nobody to date has criticised the schema as a viable and important contribution to the understanding of marital loving. In this book I have also considered the roles of parenting, kinship, and love of our neighbours.

My schema, which I will expand on in the following chapters, is based on a methodology which takes account of the first and second intimate relationships already described: the first in childhood and the second, suitably modified, in marriage. It is also built on a wide reading of the literature, over 40 years of marital counselling, and most importantly, on the experiences of my own marriage of nearly 50 years. So far its confirmation has been qualitative in the extensive affirmation of readers, listeners and discussions. Theories largely based on the interpretation of the lives of patients may have scientific critics but it is a well-attested form of psychological research, used by both Freud and Jung, and my work on loving so far belongs to this genre.

When I have written about marital love in the past, others have occasionally objected that I offer an ideal, which, however correct, remains an ideal, and that, as with theory and practice in theology, not enough is said about the difficulties. I do not believe this to be true, but I can accept that my vision of marital love, however attractive, can be intimidating and may be seen as removed from the ordinariness of daily married life with its routine of work and the stress of caring for children and running a household. In brief, there is a contrast between the loftiness of the love I present and the triviality of the everyday ordinary moment. I could be hoist by my own petard, not of being abstract, but of being too theoretical.

In response I will say that we can only cope with the boredom and routine of everyday life if we are sustained by peak moments which focus on the cement of life and relationship, namely love. But I have taken notice of my critics and am extending the discussion by including parts of a paper, 'Faithfulness and Forgiveness', which I presented in Santiago di Compostela to the International Conference of the Teams of Our Lady in 2000. This paper examines sustaining, healing, growth and sexual intercourse, which I consider to be the four pillars of marital love, describes some of the common problems and emphasises the primary Christian experience of forgiveness.

Chapter 13

Sustaining Love

The four elements of marital loving are driven by the loving energy or the libido, not in its sexual meaning, but in the psychological meaning of a life-giving force as used for example by Jung and Fairbairn. Sustaining is the first dimension of this energy. It defines the moment-to-moment life-giving that sustains and holds the couple to one another. It is made up of five principal experiences:

1. Availability – physical and emotional
2. Communication
3. Demonstration of affection
4. Affirmation
5. Resolution of conflict

which we will look at in turn.

1. Availability

Mindful of the methodology of the repetition of critical events in the first intimate relationship in the second, it is easy to see that the constant presence of the mother or a mother figure is the foundation of a child's life. Children mature through a process of gradual separation, with parents increasingly in the background. The marital relationship of couples echoes this process in its balance between availability and separation. Their availability to each other is a central factor in their love. It is experienced in being together, sitting, eating, or watching television together, going out and on holiday together and sleeping in the same room. This togetherness is a specific expression of love, and lends strength to Fairbairn's theory that our fundamental orientation of life is towards another person. Physical availability is complemented by emotional availability. Our spouse gives us the security to disclose layer after layer of ourselves, and so to become really one. At times of difficulties we unburden ourselves and our spouse shares our feelings in a loving way.

We miss this love when we do not spend enough time together, and this is a critical element for spouses when both work – it is essential to get the balance between external activities and sharing time together right. Spending too much time socialising, out drinking or in sporting activities, or even neglecting togetherness by being too busy with good causes, parish activities or family and friends, can all bring potential problems. This quality of loving is also vulnerable when spouses have jobs that take them away from each other frequently or for long periods. The ensuing sense of loss can be acute and sometimes causes difficulties that can result in marital breakdown.

Togetherness is another element in childhood where mature, loving growth consists of a balance between dependence and togetherness, and autonomy and separateness. Getting this balance right is also vital for marital love. If there is not enough separation, the child or spouse can become symbiotic, fused with the parents or spouse. Too much closeness does not allow a separate existence, and in marriage spouses can feel oppressed, experience a lack of freedom and come to feel that they are living by kind permission of their partner.

Although we think of sexual intercourse as very important and so it is, availability expressed in physical and emotional togetherness (technically called empathy) is vital for marital love. But there is togetherness without affection. Couples go out together, visit family and friends, go on holiday and so on, without any inner emotional connection. There are emotional skeletons of togetherness and inner deserts in which a couple can seem outwardly together, but are inwardly miles apart. This state can lead to affairs and finally, when enough courage is summoned, to divorce.

2. Communication

Communication has become the modern mantra for stability in

marriage. As children, love is experienced predominantly through being held, hugged, caressed and touched, all via the body, and this is a powerful communication of love. Winnicott stressed the importance of touch in childhood and it is equally vital to spouses. Christianity has had difficulties with the issue of touch and the body and its connection with eroticism. But touch is a signal of recognition, affection and reassurance. It only takes a small expenditure of energy to make us feel affirmed.

Physical touch as a communication of love is vital to spouses, but this can cause difficulties if we were brought up by parents who found touch, hugging, and holding a problem, as this can transfer itself into the second intimate relationship. There is also a gender difference. Men have greater difficulty in showing love through touch and need to appreciate touch as not specifically sexual, whereas women find this easier and want physical touch more often to feel loved than for its sexual connotation. Other methods of non-verbal communication are also important – nobody will deny how much we learn from each other by a look or a smile, by our body language, and looking at each other or away.

Verbal communication is a complex subject and has been studied extensively. It can be used for rational exposition, cognitive communication, the exchange of information and the expression of affection, emotion and anger towards one another. It is a powerful means of communication – with words we disclose ourselves, share our interests and our inner world and try to make sense of one another rationally and emotionally.

On the whole women find it easier to communicate verbally than men. They generally talk more (which men can interpret as nagging), and above all want to be listened to and feel heard. Men, on the other hand, find listening difficult. When their wives speak to them, they often interpret their words as a cry for help and a signal that there is a problem to be fixed. Men love fixing things, especially technical problems. But women often do not want to have anything fixed but to be loved by simply being heard. When men stop listening, you can see in their faces that they are mentally asking the question, 'In all these words, where is the problem that needs fixing?' Women have plenty of experience of unfinished decorating and DIY projects that overrun promised timetables, sometimes by years. When in desperation they call in a professional or finish the work themselves, their husband then asks, 'Why did you do that? I could easily have fixed it.' Women love to talk. When my daughters call, I pick up the phone and chat to them for a few minutes, but when the phone is passed to my wife, the call lasts at least half an hour!

I shall finish with the fictional story of a couple seeking a divorce before a judge. The judge asked the wife why she wanted a divorce. 'He hasn't talked to me for two years', she said. The judge turned to the husband and asked him whether this was true, and the husband replied, 'It is true, your honour. You see, I didn't want to interrupt her!'

3. Demonstration of Affection

For children, hugs, caresses and kisses are the oxygen of life. Couples want no less. Men emphasise sexual intercourse, women demonstration of affection. Many women have come to see me for counselling, accompanied by their husbands, and have complained: 'Doctor, nowadays he never tells me he loves me.' The husbands' response is generally to looked puzzled and to reply, 'I told you I loved you twenty-five years ago. Why do you want to hear it again? If I change my mind, I will let you know.' Demonstration of affection is crucial in marriage.

One way of expressing affection is humour, and many people feel loved when their partner makes them laugh. Some women in particular feel strongly that their ideal spouse is one who makes them laugh, rather than talking seriously of business, golf or sport. Children love to be tickled, played with and generally made to laugh and giggle, and in marriage, laughter can sometimes dissolve a difficult atmosphere. But humour should be handled carefully because some people can use humour as a way to express anger in disguise. Humour can hurt if it is designed to put the other spouse down or feed an air of superiority or condescension, and sarcasm can be a form of veiled criticism. When this is perceived, the offending spouse can excuse themselves by saying 'I didn't mean to hurt you. It was only a joke!' The supreme response to hurt caused by anger camouflaged as a joke is the remark, 'What's the matter with you. Can't you take a joke?'

Demonstration of loving affection is often experienced not in acts alone but in the personality of the spouse. Loving is associated with kindness, warmth, gentleness and empathy. Love is powerfully associated with feeling understood and responded to accurately.

4. Affirmation

Young children thrive on affirmation, when they are praised by parents and teachers. Hearing 'Good girl!' or 'Good boy!' is the foundation of self-esteem. Adults need affirmation no less, but this seems pathetically limited among spouses, which is a pity because it is an essential means of loving. Sadly, we often keep silent when things go well and open our mouths to criticise when things go wrong. Appreciation of loving acts and of tasks accomplished is not costly but has profound implications for marital love.

5. Resolution of Conflict

Intimacy and conflict are inevitably linked, so anger and conflict will be present in marital life and need careful handling. The presence of conflict is not a sign of marital deterioration. A quarrel is an occasion for developing a deeper understanding of something which is amiss, for finding out what has caused the hurt and trying to avoid it in the future.

There are two stages to the resolution of conflict. First, the anger has to abate. This can be done by soothing words, by a cuddle if possible, and often by an apology or the withdrawal of the offending words. (In the chapter on growth, I will explain that one of the aspects of maturity which may take a lifetime to develop is learning when to keep our mouths shut. We frequently regret hasty words.) When a young child has a temper tantrum, we try to pacify it by holding it, calming and comforting until the peak of the distress abates. Then, if possible, we move on to understanding the cause of the distress (in the case of a child, it might be losing a game, or feeling that someone has been unfair: 'It's not fair' is one of the commonest cries of child-hood and often of adulthood!).

The causes of adult quarrels are both similar and different. Commonly, people feel misunderstood, criticised unfairly, rejected and unloved, and may feel that their legitimate needs are being denied. Part of the resolution of conflict is to communicate clearly, correcting misinterpretations of what was really said or meant, and ensuring that the misunderstanding is not a projection (i.e. that what we thought we heard is not at all what the other person thought or meant). One way of doing this is to summarise at the end of the dialogue what has actually been said. This unpacks the contents.

In the midst of these arguments we find that some people are prone to losing their tempers more frequently because of frustration, lack of patience, and a tendency to react with an angry retort. These people can be acutely sensitive and can sometimes reach a stage where their anger assumes paranoid proportions and they feel constantly persecuted. Resolution of conflict comes about through a quick reduction of anger, apologies and a discussion which aims to understand and identify the roots of the conflict and to avoid one or both partners withdrawing from the relationship. Withdrawal is a more typical response of men, but if they do not engage in conflict resolution they may be pursued by their wives and withdraw further. This can create a vicious circle, leading to sulking, where the withdrawal and silence is maintained for a long time, with each side waiting for the other to apologise first.

These five principal experiences are easily recognised and described but not so easy to put into practice. However, they remain pivotal for sustaining marital love and, while there are undoubtedly other factors, counselling experience suggests that deficiencies in these areas are among the commonest causes of marital disappointment and conflict. It is commonly believed that love in all these forms is static. Men and women shrug their shoulders and comment, 'That's how he/she is. There is nothing I can do about it!' In fact, nothing could be further from the truth. We can continuously expand our sense of togetherness, improve our communication, show more affection and affirmation and develop our ability to handle conflict. Critics of marriage see it as a static life sentence. It is, of course, anything but. But we need the positive encouragement of actual living love by the Church to remind us of this.

Chapter 14

Healing and Growth

Healing

The next pillar of marital loving is healing. Such ordinary healing is by its very nature invisible, and is not the active result of seeking help; few marital counsellors write about it or even recognise it. As a recipient of healing in my own marriage from my very loving wife, my attention has been drawn to it repeatedly. Once aware of its presence, you can begin to see it all around you, and others acknowledge it when it is drawn to their attention. Healing is, of course, central to adult therapy within counselling, but I maintain that the processes of adult therapy are a constant, unnoticed presence in so-called 'normal' ordinary marriage. Returning to the pages of Vatican II:

> Thus a man and a woman who by the marriage covenant of conjugal love are no longer two but one flesh render mutual help and service to each other through an intimate union of their persons and of their acts . . . This love is an eminently human one since it is directed from one person to another through an affection of the will. It involves the good of the whole person . . . This the Lord had judged worthy of special gifts, healing, perfecting (growth) and exalting gifts of grace and of charity.[1]

My aim is to translate this theology into a concrete reality for marital love, and I am saddened to find as I go round lecturing how few priests and married couples have read these pages.

Soon after we marry, sometimes very soon, we discover that the person we idealised is far from perfect, and we may even detect this when we are courting. I refer here not to huge imperfections, but to common personality difficulties. We may begin to discern that our spouse is prone to lack of self-esteem, lack of confidence or a tendency to feel unlovable; inclined to feel easily rejected and criticised; finds it difficult to register love and retain it; repeatedly needs reassurance; feels insecure, excessively anxious or unsure of themselves; is over-assertive, argumentative, or reticent, apologetic and silent. These are not the serious problems of aggression, morbid jealousy, paranoid tendencies and the extremes of gambling, alcoholism and drug addiction, but the ordinary problems which most people struggle with, and which I call 'wounds'. We are all wounded people in some ways, both spiritually and psychologically, and the two often overlap.

From previous chapters, it will be seen that most of these wounds are psychologically determined. The biggest problems may have a genetic cause: indeed all of them, mild and severe, may be the result of a mixture of nurture and nature. These wounds emerge early in the marriage and it is crucial that they are properly dealt with. In the past, and sometimes in the present, we have used the common psychological device of blaming the wounded person. Since most of these wounds are a result of lack of love in childhood and result in attention-seeking behaviour, we often call these people self-centred, egotistical and selfish. In fact they are psychologically traumatised. Some people will ask, 'What about sin and its consequences in terms of selfishness, pride, greed, and so on?' I do not deny the presence of sin but I believe that, even if we use this concept as a way of describing the root of difficult behaviour, it does not change my position that the consequences of sin need a human means of expressing themselves. I really believe that the more likely explanation is that the psychological root of problem behaviour comes from a shortage of love.

The healing that is widespread in marriage comes not from attacking the sufferer because we do not know what else to do, but from using John's concept of avoiding punishment. Punishment is associated with fear and in fear there is an absence of love (1 John 4:18). The loving response is not to judge people adversely, but to try to understand the causes of their wounds by recognising their infantile, child-like difficulties and the damaging impact of their mishandling. A simple form of healing is that we replace lack of love with its opposite. To their insecurity we give an abundance of reassurance, to their lack of confidence a wealth of affirmation. This process is simple to understand and goes on all the time in good marriages.

But healing can be understood in three other ways. I have mentioned Freud's concept of transference, where within a close intimate relationship we return and reclaim our childhood traumas, discern the patterns of love or lack of it and learn to make the distinction between our parental figures and our adult spouse. By intuitive moments of insight, we render the unconscious conscious and accept what belongs to us and what is our responsibility.

Following the same line of thought, Winnicott conceived the idea of the false self, the 'nice' appearance we present publicly while hiding our real self which we do not dare to show. Part of the healing process is to shift as much as we can from the false to the real, both for ourselves and for our spouse, and thus to become more genuine people. How we choose to do this is vital. We can choose to blame, using the phrase that reverberates through the world of intimate relationships, 'The trouble with you is . . .' This is an accusatory approach, and a favourite of sin-oriented religion. Alternatively, and far more lovingly, we can be non-judgemental, identify the problem as a wound and not a fault, try to uncover the parental or institutional deprivation behind its presence, and attempt to overcome it with a combination of personal growth and the support of a loving spouse.

The third understanding of healing is based on cognitive psychology: that is, helping the spouse to replace their negative image of themselves. The beliefs, 'I am no good!', 'I can't do or achieve anything useful', 'Nothing good ever happens to me', 'I am a destructive person' and 'I can't love', all need challenging and replacing by positive thoughts. One of the standard therapeutic techniques of cognitive psychology, which we all do in a modified form, is by replying to all these negative remarks by saying, 'No, you are not . . .' But we often fail to follow this up with positive praise such as, 'Just look at what you have achieved!' Of course we can all be a little awful at times and, as the psychiatrist whose patient said, 'Doctor, I feel inferior' replied, 'I agree – you are inferior!', sometimes we must agree with our spouse!

Clearly loving is not easy, but it should be our aim to try continuously, round the clock, and to practise these various ways of healing. Because loving is difficult and requires patience and persistence, we have a tendency to substitute the shortcut of rules for love, and to build a framework to limit the damage. But as Christians, we are not here for damage limitation, but to accept the evangelical request, 'You must therefore set no bounds to your love, just as your heavenly Father sets none to his' (Matt. 5:48).

So far, the healing possibilities appear simple, and indeed I am convinced they are widely practised without realising that spouses are acting as therapists, but (and it is a big 'but') most of these healing practices work when there is a wounded spouse living with a much less damaged person, or, more commonly, with a spouse who has different problems. When both spouses are seriously and similarly wounded, for example when they are both starving for love, there is a very real problem.

I have mentioned in detail these wounds because they are the commonest reasons for marital conflict and ultimately divorce. Equally, I have described healing at length because I am convinced that it is widely present in millions of homes and offers one of the most optimistic possibilities for the doom-and-gloom scenario of marriage in contemporary society. The latter is inclined to handle these problems, particularly if they are persistent, by opting out and looking for a second more successful relationship. There is no doubt that a few second marriages can be successful, but sadly one set of problems is usually replaced by another. Another option is to feel that we have burned our fingers and to choose the single state permanently. Statistics show a higher rate of failure for second marriages and an increasing population of single people.

It is my view that Christianity fails seriously in its advocacy of marriage by not proclaiming loudly the reality of healing within it, and that there is more healing in the totality of marriage than in all the healing achievements of psychiatric couches of the world. This is one of the many graces of love of this Sacrament, together with many other unproclaimed positive effects on mental and physical health, self-esteem, security, enhanced well-being and positive impact on children. Nevertheless, Christianity remains a poor and unconvincing advocate of marriage, and for a long time saw marriage merely as giving permission for sex and the creation of children. Children are, of course, marvellous, but, in a world dominated by the realisation and promotion of our own personal potential, we are failing by not proclaiming loudly that this is precisely what marriage offers.

The critics of marriage see it as a lifetime jail sentence, but this view ignores the secure base that it offers for the best realisation of our own potential. We need the conditions of continuity, predictability and reliability, which are precisely the best conditions for the loving education of children and, ultimately, the best conditions for marital stability, love and happiness. This is the life-long marriage that Christianity advocates but the Church needs a great deal of informed awareness and skilled presentation to persuade young people of this, although they repeatedly claim in surveys that they want marriage and family. Unfortunately the Catholic Church is better known for its opposition to pre-marital sex, contraception, abortion, adultery and divorce than for advocating in detail the positive assets of marriage. Once again we need to move from the negative to the positive, from the 'Don't' to the 'Do', from prohibitive rules to affirmative love.

Growth

Healing is the infrastructure to the growth that is a feature of marital love, but is hardly mentioned in marital studies. It is well known that physical growth and the development of the IQ finishes at around the middle of the second decade. However, we continue to mature emotionally. Jung's psychology, for example, outlines a powerful phase of emotional development in the second half of life. What Jung calls 'individuation' is a process of integrating archetypes, reconciling the collective unconscious with the individual unconscious, which includes our shadow, and moving from the persona or false self to the real self. This brief description cannot do justice to the richness of Jung's psychology (see Chapter 27), but is a reminder of the fact that there is a continuation of the growth of the personality between Freud's theories on the first half of life and Jung's on the second. This will be further discussed in the chapter on loving ourselves and our neighbours. We can more easily illustrate the growth of the personality in terms of intelligence. As we mature we move from intelligence to wisdom, and our spouse can contribute to this process by loving us, acting as a mirror for us, and helping us to disclose the truth about ourselves.

Another way of defining growth is in our emotional movement from dependence, through independence to interdependence, which is a universal phenomenon. Some people do not reach mature independence until late in life and once again this can be facilitated by the spouse. Then there is the growth of creativity. In the course of our lives we can develop previously hidden talents in a whole range of areas such as gardening, cooking and hobbies, and in middle age we may change jobs or take a new and important direction in our lives. In all these areas the spouse can encourage and facilitate or discourage by saying, 'You can't do that!' A spouse who stifles emerging qualities in their partner may damage the relationship to the point where this prompts a divorce. On the other hand, the partner seeking the conditions for a new creativity may find in their partner someone who listens, encourages and motivates.

We can grow in our capacity to love in all the ways I have already shown, and this can be illustrated by the most ordinary example: by learning when to keep our mouth shut and when to open it! It sounds simple but it takes a lifetime to achieve. With the passage of time, we discover more about the inner world of our spouse, and love them more by responding more accurately to who they are, and the wounds they carry which need time to unravel and be healed. We also learn to trust them enough to reveal ourselves, as we uncover more and more of who we are, descending into our depths and finding out things about ourselves that we never knew or understood. All these things can be discovered and expressed in the love of a spouse who is patient, receptive, open, supportive, not easily shocked, and always unconditionally accepting.

At the heart of growth is not only the acquisition of new skills but the sense of continuity that allows us to penetrate the successive layers of ourselves and recognise them as they surface. Critics of this affirmation of permanency in marriage would say that we can grow just as well by entering into a new relationship which gives us a fresh possibility or second chance to understand who we are. This is true, but we pay the price of losing all the effort we have put into our first relationship, and face the problems of an encounter of a new stranger and the work we have to do afresh. Last, but not least, comes the adverse impact on our children.

The concept of marital growth has scarcely been developed in society, with the exception of common observations on the impact of the mid-life crisis, the menopause and the death of parents. At a personal level we can all grow through the impact of illness, social adversity, job changes, unemployment and so on. All these are important but the growth of our inner world and its profound impact on ourselves and others have yet to be widely appreciated.

What is certain is that the presence of a sensitive, perceptive, responsive, unconditionally loving spouse is an immense facilitating gift. Healing and growth teach us to be better lovers, not only in the usual sexual meaning of the word, but as lovers of the whole of ourselves, our partner and our children. In this love we realise our full potential of the image of God within us and actualise the presence of a God who is love. If only Christianity could project widely both amongst the young and the not so young the image of marriage proclaimed in the last two chapters, we would have a language which would make real the teaching of Vatican II and become an effective instrument for evangelisation.

Chapter 15

Sexual Intercourse

I come now to the fourth and last pillar of marital love, namely sexual intercourse. I have written a whole book, *Let's Make Love*,[1] devoted to this topic which gives a lengthy examination of the subject, including a detailed analysis of my rejection of *Humanae Vitae*, the scriptural basis for my enthusiastic belief in the sacredness of intercourse, and a brief history of the reasons for Christianity's negative approach to it. To me, a vital issue is the link of sexual intercourse with love. This reality has only been embraced by the whole of Christianity in the last century, and has been particularly expressed in the Roman Catholic Church by the Second Vatican Council. I quote from the pages of the Council:

> This love (marital love) is uniquely expressed and perfected through the marital act. The actions within marriage by which the couple are united intimately and chastely are noble and worthy ones. Expressed in a manner which is truly human, these actions signify and promote the mutual self-giving by which spouses enrich each other with a joyful and thankful will.[2]

Once again this theological language needs to be translated into the meaningful living love that it proclaims. Summarising my book, I describe sexual intercourse as first of all being the consummation of sustaining, healing and growth. We often desire to make love after we have spent time together, communicated effectively, demonstrated loving affection, affirmed each other or resolved conflict. (This generally applies more to the woman, whose desire to make love can be prompted by an affectionate encounter, rather than to the man who is prompted to discharge libidinal drives, but of course the reverse can also be true.) Thus my first understanding of the meaning of sexual intercourse is an act of love that is the fulfilment and consummation of these five experiences (and of course many others). The consummation of sustaining also accompanies healing and growth.

I also argue that the well-recognised pleasure of sexual intercourse is not a sufficient explanation of its meaning. Important as the orgasm is, its meaning is much more extensive than its physical aspects. The associated pleasure is a body language, a concept that John Paul II has described,[4] but I believe he has reached the wrong conclusions with regards to contraception. Quite independently, I have pursued the idea of sexual intercourse as a language in psychological terms.

If the couple are talking with their bodies, what are they saying to each other, consciously or unconsciously? I believe they are saying at least five things.

1. They are saying to each other, 'You are the most important person in my life, the person who I recognise, want, need and appreciate.' This is a most powerful affirmation of the identity of the spouse.
2. In the process of sexual intercourse, the man confirms most powerfully the femininity of the woman and she her husband's masculinity. It is a most powerful affirmation of their sexual identity. (At this point homosexuality and heterosexuality diverge.)
3. I have already referred to the fact that spouses quarrel, hurt one another and cause pain. Usually they forgive and forget quickly but sometimes the pain is deep and lasts a long time. After an interval, sex often breaks the barrier of alienation. Here it is an act of reconciliation.
4. Deep in ourselves we long to feel that we are wanted. It is commonly agreed that sexual intercourse is a moment for joyful play and the experience of pleasure. It is all this but, in fact, the invitation to intercourse is one of the most powerful signals to show us that we are wanted. It is a recurrent act of faith, hope and love in one another, independent of the physical and psychological outcome.
5. Finally, it is one of the most powerful ways of saying 'Thank you!

Thank you for being with me yesterday, today, and hopefully tomorrow.'

Although the more successful the orgasm is, the more complete these personal meanings become, they are present independent of the intensity of the pleasure. Apart from its pleasurable meaning, it is one of the most important ways of translating the 'I-Thou' encounter, and this happens independently of the frequency of the act, which has become the obsessional preoccupation of the world.

Finally, there is the spiritual dimension. If one couples the scriptural passages of Genesis about Yahweh finding all he had created not only good but very good (Gen. 1:31) with the Song of Songs and other passages, sexual intercourse undoubtedly becomes a sacred act. For me, it is the central and recurrent act of prayer in marriage. According to Vatican II, it is intimately linked with love and in my book[5] I have described intercourse as an 'act of love'. According to St John 'God is love' (1 John 4:8). It is rarely appreciated that when couples make love they reach the very centre of the Godhead.

The connection with the Godhead goes further. Sexual intercourse is an act that unites into one two separate persons who, with their interpersonal love, become a threesome that becomes one, and at the same time the persons are completely separate. In fact I am symbolically describing the Trinity, the very essence of our faith. Sexual intercourse is one of the most powerful symbols of the Trinity. In intercourse we move truly close to God. The combination of the words of Genesis, St John's teaching and the Trinitarian symbolism of intercourse gives it a sacredness which makes a mockery of the hostility to sex in the tradition of the Church.

It can now be seen that the real answer to *Humanae Vitae* goes well beyond biology and openness to life into the realm of theology. Given the understanding of marital love in terms of sustaining, healing and growth, it is an act in which every time the couple make love they give life to each other and occasionally new life will arise as a product of this. This definition is consistent with all I have said about marital love and its total internal meaning. It is consonant with its biological background potentiality which restricts the woman's fertility to a few days in the monthly cycle. It is biologically impossible for every act of love to be open to new life and intercourse, of course, continues after the menopause. A woman would have had great difficulty in writing *Humanae Vitae* for, however connected she is with procreation, she intuitively understands the impossibility of its teaching.

This description of sexual intercourse completes the four pillars of my understanding of love in marriage. I offer it, as I have constantly offered it, for consideration by the people of God as my contribution to the understanding of Vatican II's definition of marriage as a 'community of life and love'. I have concentrated on marriage but the issues of sustaining, healing and growth apply widely to all intimate human relationships of love.

Chapter 16

Forgiveness

In sustaining, healing, growth and sexual intercourse we have positive goals to aim for, but we fail all the time. God knows this and he sent his only Son to rescue us from our failures to love enough. In our Christian thinking, we consider the answer to these failures as forgiveness, and so it is. Forgiveness is the act and behaviour through which we take away our anger and hurt towards the person who has let us down. Very often the notion of forgiveness stops there but, as I will show, it must not. Forgiveness should elicit a resolve from the person forgiven to do better in the future and to avoid repeating the hurt. Of course the hurt usually goes but the memory may remain for a long time, sometimes a lifetime. Forgiveness is so important that Jesus commanded us to forgive even our enemies (Matt. 5:44).

But forgiveness is not a simple process. When we are offended, how angry and hurt we become depends on the sensitivity of our personality. Some people who have been previously traumatised have a low threshold to hurt and experience a lot of pain after what appears to be a trivial matter. It is no use saying to our spouse that they should not be offended, interpreting it as trivial, and dismissing their experience. We must recognise the genuine level of their sensitivity and accept that some people are easily hurt. If so, they may take some time to recover. People are in the habit of saying, 'I said sorry. What else do you want me to do?', but the wound may be deep and wide, and when we apologise, we must not always expect instant reconciliation, although we will yearn for it because as children we did not want to be too long out in the cold beyond the warmth of our parents' acceptance.

On the other hand, the attitude, 'Let them sweat it out' is not

---

loving. Forgiveness has a time element, and we can punish our partner by keeping them at a distance and withholding our apology. Apologies must not only be deeply felt but also, in the traditional language of theology, we must show a sincere desire to repent and a firm purpose of amendment: that is, a desire to learn from our offence, discover what went wrong and try to avoid repeating it.

So what can we do when we fall short of our sustaining love? The first element I have already mentioned here is our availability. Failure here is a common problem in modern society. Often both partners work and children make demands, leaving the couple with little time for togetherness. We must be conscious of the need for availability to each other. We can forgive its momentary lapses but, in the long term, the corollary to forgiveness is the desire, determination and resolution to be with our spouse. What we often have to forgive is not the occasional lack of presence in each other's life but, more seriously, we have to forgive, or at least try to understand, the fact that our partner finds it difficult to be in our company. Work is often a reason, but it can also be an excuse. We need to go beyond forgiveness to try to understand what we are doing that may repel our partner. Do we take enough care with our appearance, or take time to accommodate our partner's interests? A marriage in which the husband is mad on football and the wife on the theatre or other hobbies, needs determined compromise. What outings can we embark on together? If our partner finds it difficult to be with us, beyond forgiveness, healing requires that we find out what may be wrong with us. It is always too easy to blame the other spouse.

After availability comes communication where there is much to forgive and to change. Do we talk too much and bore our spouse? Do we repeat the same stories or do we talk too little? Are we good listeners? Do we just wait for our partner to stop talking so that we can start? Do we listen carefully, not only to understand the rational meaning of their words, but also to discern their feelings? Do we interrupt too often? Tolerance, forgiveness and healing are needed in which we make an effort to understand and respond to each other's style of communication. Are we the type of husband who thinks, 'I don't mind her having the last word. In fact I wait for it to arrive in eagerness!'

When it comes to demonstration of affection, are we aware that our wife wants to be kissed, hugged and caressed at times other than sexual intercourse? Non-sexual affection is a key to love. As a partner, when we need affection and it is not available, do we put up with the deprivation and become increasingly resentful or do we insist that change takes place? We can endure and inwardly seethe but how are things going to change if we do not communicate with our spouse?

Are we the type of person who keeps our mouth shut when things go well without appreciation and opens it to criticise when things go wrong? Jesus himself needed affirmation and received it at his Baptism and Transfiguration. What are we doing to ensure that we don't neglect to affirm our spouse?

Resolution of conflict is an essential aftermath of forgiveness. We must make sure that we not only forgive those who have hurt us but also try to understand the cause of the conflict and avoid repetition. It is easy to move from one reconciliation to another without dealing with the root of the problem. While Jesus' answer to how often we have to forgive (Matt. 18:21–22) is an ideal model, human patience has its limitations and this is another trigger for divorce. In all forgiveness it is essential that we do not adopt a superior attitude, feeling smug about our magnanimity. In forgiveness we have to touch the hurt heart of the offender.

I have already mentioned in detail the central role of healing. God heals continuously in that he restores our relationship with him as we fail repeatedly through sin. Our parents heal us throughout our childhood as we fall short of physical and social integrity. Spouses have to heal each other repeatedly. Healing is a particular expression of loving faithfulness. We do not have to heal only sexual unfaithfulness. The wounds of our spouse may be particularly tiresome, tedious and repetitive. They can appear selfish, self-centred and egotistical. They may seem always to put themselves first but, as we have seen, they may be simply reacting out of their hunger for love.

Our spouse's offences are often small matters which can cause immense irritation. They may be habitually late, avoid our relatives and ignore our requests for change. What appears to be a deliberate avoiding of change may be, and usually is, the result of their psychological wounds. Sometimes there are more serious problems such as drinking too much or aggressive behaviour (domestic violence is common the world over). The wounded person is conditioned in their patterns of behaviour. They may get easily angry, even violent, or they may be mean and miserly, sulking and withdrawn. Whatever their problem, it persists and persists. We may become accustomed to it, tolerant, forgiving, or may give up and separate or divorce.

Forgiveness within the trivia of everyday life is much more difficult to achieve. We have to love our wounded spouse by being patient for a long time with their deficiencies and yet never giving up hope of change. How long can we tolerate their behaviour? The Christian response to this question is fundamentally different from the secular one. I am often asked by spouses how long they should wait before they depart. The Christian answer is ideally forever. In practice, the spouse should wait as long as possible, with the important caveat that they must leave if they are in danger of grave and intense emotional and/or physical damage. One very experienced priest, answering this question, said, 'We must love for better and for worse but not for impossible.' We should never give up hope and the most fruitful way of achieving this is by constantly noticing every little effort to change for the better and both recognising and appreciating this.

For Christianity, the response, 'Too little, too late' has no place in a loving relationship. The wounded person is a victim of their conditioned patterns of trauma and it is easier for them to repeat the problematic behaviour that to avoid it, simply because they are familiar with it, sometimes since childhood. There are people who as I said are always late, untidy, unreliable, and always have an excuse for their behaviour. Forgiveness is hard in the face of such persistent irritation and pain. In the past what appeared to be forgiveness was a compulsory response because people had no choice. Now they have, and women in particular choose to vote with their feet – 75 per cent of petitions for divorce in Britain are filed by women. It is no good shouting about the scourge of divorce if we do not go to the roots of the problem and take preventive action.

The Christian characteristic of forgiveness is never giving up, as far as is humanly possible, and always encouraging change. There is of course a world of difference between encouraging change and persistent negative criticism. We may get fed up, and we often do, with the behaviour of our spouse but it is when we are at our lowest that we have to start again.

Another way of being lovingly faithful is by helping each other to grow, to realise our potential, to increase our capacity to love, and to make real the image of God in each other. We need to be accurately attentive to each other's needs. We need to love each other by safeguarding one another's material needs, such as food, housing and money, and by providing a secure base for the other to grow and mature. Spouses grow in adult life, socially, emotionally and cognitively. As I have already mentioned, they grow by becoming independent, taking the initiative, becoming creative, and acquiring new skills and new understanding. The partner facilitates this growth by being encouraging and supportive. It is not loving to say, 'I wouldn't even try that. You can't do that. You can dream away. I bet you anything you can't do it.' Betting is not safe because it raises the determination to do the impossible!

Forgiveness with growth is especially needed when we have moved forward in some way and our spouse is marking time and lagging behind. We may have gained confidence and want to be adventurous while our spouse is stuck with the old ways and is unwilling to contemplate change. The unequal growth and change between spouses means that forgiveness sometimes requires that we tolerate the inability of our spouse to keep up with us while we keep on urging change.

Occasionally, it is the constant prodding by our partner that irritates. Our spouse may see our behaviour as primarily an intellectual excuse: 'If you loved me, you would do this or that for me!' Some people persist in the belief that all that is needed is a rational change of the will. If only things were that easy! Such people find it very difficult to believe that emotion and feelings are involved in faults laid down long ago. They come to the conclusion that we are deliberately not trying to change when in fact we are trying our best but find it very difficult. How often do we hear: 'He/she does it deliberately to annoy me.' Forgiveness is needed in these circumstances for the blindness of our spouse. We are reminded of the words of Jesus, 'Forgive them; they do not know what they are doing' (Luke 23:34). Often we need to forgive the behaviour of our spouse when they hurt not through malice but through ignorance. In psychological terms, it is the operation of their unconscious, and we often hear the words 'I didn't mean it.' We cannot all become psychiatrists in order to understand such behaviour, but we can all try not to jump to bad, malicious, conclusions.

At the heart of forgiveness is sexual unity. In the passage on sexual intercourse, I referred to the fact that love-making is a body language that conveys personal love. What is often forgotten is that, if this is true, the quality of love-making must be treated with the utmost seriousness, both physically and emotionally. I have described the details in *Let's Make Love*[6] but, in summary, we must pay attention to the atmosphere preceding love-making and the quality of touch. We must demonstrate our affection and take great care to synchronise orgasm as far as possible so that both partners enjoy it. The latter can be a problem for men. The quality of the act is intimately affected by selfishness. This selfishness is more than genital dysfunction. It may be that our spouse has been sexually hurt in the past and finds it difficult to make love. It may be that they desire more or less sex than we do. It may be that they are a poor lover and insensitive to our needs.

We must be careful how we forgive and seek change in sexual matters because in this area we are our most sensitive and vulnerable selves. By implication, by commenting on the poor technique of our partner, we may be dismissing their whole approach to loving, for the body is central and operates through the whole personality. In rejecting the physical, we may be rejecting the whole person. So when things go wrong sexually, we have to be gentle, patient, tolerant and show how things can improve, without ever reducing the level of love and respect for our spouse.

The ultimate forgiveness in sexual matters is needed for adultery, which is still common. In our society, despite its permissiveness, adultery is still taken seriously and is considered as the ultimate betrayal. We can be unfaithful to our spouse in many ways, as I have described above, but if we commit adultery we put their trust in our love in peril. In forgiving adultery, which we must do, we have to consider its varying types and their meaning.

In my clinical experience I have divided adultery into three forms. The first of these is the one-night stand, usually involving spouses who are away from home for short periods of time on business, on courses, at conferences or even on holiday. It is interpreted as, and would appear to be, an opportunity for physical sex but it can often be a way of coping with the pain of loneliness and the need for human contact. This type of adultery is not usually a threat to the marriage.

Next there is the affair that continues for weeks or months but is usually of short duration. Often the husband or wife confesses and there is a quarrel. Once again these short-term affairs are painful but need not be a threat to the marriage and both forgiveness and reconciliation can follow. Thirdly, there is the affair that continues for a long time, signalling a move to a new emotional commitment and resulting in the breakdown of the marriage.

Why do men and women commit adultery? The usual answer given is because of the pleasure of sex but this is an insufficient explanation. Men may do so for sex more often than women, especially when it is not available at home, while for women emotional reasons may predominate. Women can be tempted to have affairs if they are short of affection, feel unloved, or want to discover another aspect of their personality that is unavailable with their spouse, or if they suffer from a lack of self-esteem which is boosted when they feel wanted and appreciated in an affair. Both men and women can be simply bored.

Adultery is a betrayal. It is a transfer of love from the spouse to a third party. In the context of what I have said about the meaning of sexual intercourse, it is the displacement of personal affirmation from the spouse to another. There is a loss of identity and love. The commonest hurt of all adultery is a loss of trust. The intimate security of togetherness is fractured. The restoration of trust after an affair can take time but in all human societies adultery should not be a case for the breakdown of marriage but an occasion for forgiveness. Forgiveness, however, is not enough. Adultery is a crisis and an opportunity for the spouses to examine their lives. The adulterer should explore what he or she is trying to get out of the affair and see whether what is missing in the marriage can be achieved within it. Even this is not enough. The 'so-called' innocent party may have been partly responsible for the adultery by acts of omission or commission that drove their partner into the affair.

Adultery is an occasion to take stock of the marital situation, socially, emotionally and sexually. It is a warning that all is not well with the marriage, and that it is in need of repair and restructuring.

An examination of the reasons of the infidelity is essential, with correction and healing to follow. Christianity has to learn that, in relationships, forgiveness is essential but not always enough. If it is seen as the first step not the last, then forgiveness truly begins to heal.

Adultery is a case *par excellence* of betrayal and loss of trust, but all the wounding surrounding sustaining, healing and growth is a gradual erosion of trust and love. It is this gradual erosion that slowly empties the coffers of love until one day, imperceptibly, they become totally empty. This is why it is imperative that forgiveness is followed by repair so that love can be rekindled.

Human relationships of intimate love have no fuel gauge telling us where we are in life's tank of love and, if we are not careful, the indicator will suddenly move to 'empty'. The frequency of conflict and forgiveness is a warning measure of the quality of our relationship. Relationships of love are not cars that can be bought and sold. When we face our Creator, it will be good if we can have the advertisement 'One careful owner'!

Chapter 17

Defining Maturity

I have no professional educational qualifications, and I leave the imparting of knowledge to those who have. I approach this topic from the point of view of an adult psychiatrist, much of whose ordinary work is generated by the presence of intelligence and the relative absence of maturity and the ability to develop affectionate bonds dealt with in this chapter and the next.

One of the biggest problems facing advanced Western societies is the emphasis on the acquisition and implementation of knowledge at the expense of education for emotional maturity. The Catholic Church in particular has been obsessed with knowledge as the basis for practising the good life of faith. During my schooldays, and for many years afterwards, the Catechism reigned supreme. In many ways it still does, reflecting the belief that a combination of knowing the faith and applying appropriate rules is the basis for implementing the Christian life against a background of liturgy, prayer and Sacraments. Sadly, it is nothing of the sort. A rational expression of faith, particularly through philosophy, which operates with reason and the law book, but without the heart (feelings and emotions), is a recipe for discord between the inner and the outer self and can lead to hypocrisy. The consequent lack of perceived integrity is the fuel of the newspapers and the media, and has helped to perpetuate an atmosphere of disbelief in anything that is good, genuine and really reflects God. Although dogmatic formulae, integrated with law and obedience to rules, are important, integrity understood as the cohesive expression of body, mind and heart is more important, and reflects more accurately what Jesus stood for.

In the terms of this book, the conjunction between mind and heart

---

111

is of supreme importance. Jesus, the first and most effective psychiatrist, had this to say with reference to cleanliness and uncleanliness:

> 'Can't you see that whatever goes into the mouth passes through the stomach and is discharged into the sewer? But whatever comes out of the mouth comes from the heart and it is this that makes someone unclean. For from the heart comes evil intentions: murder, adultery, fornication, theft, perjury, slander. These are the things that make a person unclean. But eating with unwashed hands does not make anyone unclean.' (Matt. 15:17–20)

This quotation emphasises the heart as the supreme seat of love. One of the great advances of moral theology in the aftermath of Vatican II has been the shift of emphasis from individual acts to the whole person. For the rest of this chapter I want to look at maturity, which is probably one of the most difficult psychological concepts to understand. It is, however, of fundamental importance to human life, particularly as, although it has an input in every aspect of life, it is clearly the most determining element in the success of intimate personal relationships. Having spent nearly 40 years working with married couples, there is no doubt in my mind that the single most important factor in a marriage's stability is the maturity of the couple. The same applies in friendships and working relationships, in vocations such as the priesthood, and indeed in any undertaking in which we invest our efforts.

Why do we find it so hard to define maturity, yet so easy to recognise it when we see it? The reason is that its point of reference is so wide that there is no easy comprehensive definition or understanding of its meaning. We start with the Ten Commandments and here we have a category of universal moral principles. We then have the Scriptures where we find the concepts of love, peace, justice and sacrifice, to the point of giving up one's life for the sake of love. In everyday life, martyrdom is not often required but with every moment of altruism and generosity, forgiveness, love and compassion, we reach the pinnacles of human endeavour.

Moving on to dynamic psychology, in Freud we encounter sexuality and aggression and in Object Relations psychology the basis of human love. Rules also predominate both in Scripture and in the cognitive psychology of Piaget and Kohlberg. All these operate within a system of dynamic development in which we shift from infancy, through separation from parents and to another intimate relationship (for most of us) and to friendship (for everyone). So maturity has to take account of the constraints of our make-up, how we exercise them, and the stage of our development. Independent of faith, how the various elements come together under the umbrella of love is where, in Christian terms, God and the perfection of his image in us through love are to be found.

Assembling all this into a meaningful and simple order is a gigantic task and, however we do it, we are open to criticism. For example, in the above description, sociologists will decry the absence of social factors and their influence. Clearly human relationships stand out as of paramount importance in marriage, friendship, kinship and, in the case of marriage, for no other reason than that stable relationships are the foundation of raising children as loving secure people.

We start off with the philosophical and theological distinction of an 'I-Thou' relationship and an 'I-It' encounter. Buber spelled out the distinction between the two, with the 'I-Thou' relationship calling overwhelmingly for special consideration. To reiterate my first wide generalisation, I believe that there is a deficiency in Western society, in that since Greek times we have stressed intellectual ability as the pinnacle of achievement. This is now observed in schools, with their emphasis on exam results, and in higher education. Intellectual achievement, with its abstract, analytical, logical, sequential, predictive attributes, relies heavily on philosophy and has much to commend it, but it can be deficient in appreciating the reality of living experience and the love of the Kingdom of God. This rational, analytical approach has had a great impact on theology, particularly Thomistic theology, and is both one of the glories and one of the deficiencies of the Catholic Church.

As a psychiatrist, I repeatedly see the difficulties in the combination of intellect, even high intellect, with an immature ability to relate to people. I believe this is a contributory factor to the marital breakdown which affects between 40 and 50 per cent of marriages in Britain and the USA. This discrepancy is also present in the instincts that run riot in alcoholism, addiction, gambling and failures in sexual and personal relationships that can destroy the intimate 'other' or even lead to their suicide. When the majority of people face up to the attempted suicide of a loved one (attempted suicides can run into hundreds of thousands), or to the trauma of suicide itself, they are often at a loss to understand the reasons. These are primarily found in a relational and emotional immaturity that is completely unrelated to any abstract philosophical thinking.

My second wide generalisation about maturity is that at the heart of being human is a gradual separation between the child and the parents, each progressive stage carrying the appropriate physical, intellectual, cognitive, emotional and spiritual development. One of the most useful ways of understanding immaturity is to consider it as functioning as an earlier stage of development, particularly emotionally, at a later chronological age. Our commonest understanding of immaturity is when we call someone a child, and say they are acting like a child or having child-like characteristics while presenting as a so-called adult. We know that there is a child in all of us. What matters is the age of that child and how much of our life it controls, how much it dominates and whether people recognise its presence and make due corrective allowances for it.

Another measure of maturity is the choices we make in relationships, and what kind of characteristics we are looking for in the selection of a spouse, friends, employment, and even a vocation to the priesthood. If we go for intellectual excellence at the expense of emotional qualities, and mind at the expense of heart, in marriage in particular, the consequences can be dire, and the same applies for spiritual leaders. At the interpersonal emotional level, positive feelings are generated by gentleness, warmth, kindness, generosity, care, and concern. Although intellectual and management skills are important for business, we now realise that these personal attributes are also of equal importance. There is no doubt that these characteristics are important in intimate loving relationships, and in these we are staring at the determinants of love.

So far I have dealt mainly with emotional maturity. I also have something to say about cognitive maturity. This concerns not only the intellect but also everyday issues of justice, fairness, responsibility, reciprocity and rules. Piaget and Kohlberg based their research on the moral development of children on watching them playing in neutral forms of games and offering scenarios that require moral judgements. As mentioned previously, it appears that we move on a scale of maturity from a phase of no rules, through blind obedience to rules (in which the Church I grew up in was stuck), the evaluation of rules depending on the circumstances, autonomy from rules, altruism and, finally, in Christian terms, to the absolute principle of love of our neighbour that may even require the giving up of our lives, or, as we see in the world today, for a cause.

In summary, maturity is about the maximum realisation of our potential in being, thought and action. It is about the acquisition, possession, retention and giving of ourselves that makes up our physical, social, intellectual and emotional identity. Maturity is ultimately about the quality of our availability, and its ultimate expression is Jesus Christ. It is certainly not about what Western society considers excellence in one area, whether it is intellectual ability or abstract thought, or about what I was brought up with in the Church, namely obedience to rules. The philosopher, the intellectual, the artist and the universally admired figures of excellence who offer the world ideas and other skills are, of course, essential but they may be, and often are, emotionally and relationally immature people with all the adverse consequences that entails. The consummation of maturity in Christian terms is ultimately the depth of authentic love.

In psychiatry, one discovers that society's figures of authority such as lawyers, judges, politicians and top business people can be subject to violent and immature behaviour, prejudices and very disturbed emotions. In Christianity, the echelons of the hierarchy in all denominations may be intellectually and organisationally excellent (though this is not always the case!) but emotionally and sexually very immature. The history of Christianity in all denominations shows this all too well, but the current example in the Roman Catholic Church, of sexual abuse by the clergy, reminds us that authority is much more than a matter of hierarchical status and adherence to rules. It is rather a discernment of the free and mature person who arrives at the good in an autonomous way, operates through conscience and love, and categorically places service and not power at the forefront.

I will finish with a particular application to the Catholic Church. This Church offers Christian truths as it sees them and continues to stress obedience and conformity to rules. In my opinion, it has the fatal tendency to put law, all law, at the centre and love at the periphery. This attitude has enormous implications. Obedience to authority is important but has two dangers. Firstly, it runs the risk of stopping us thinking for ourselves and of enhancing the child in us, and so puts us in danger of operating an infantile Church. Obedience is linked with dependence, and is essentially a characteristic of living by kind permission of others.

Linked with this dependence is another risk that Freud and others have pointed out: that we make God into a projected father figure of authority and protection instead of into the God who is love described by St John. A Church living in an atmosphere of blind hierarchical obedience attracts people who are immature and whose identity depends on this type of structure. At present this attracts vocations from people whose personalities are immature and dependent, who want to be priests for the support (unconsciously) it gives to their immaturity, and people, vehemently conservative, who repeatedly scream at innovation, because their personality and identity is linked with the preservation of an authoritarian structure and the status quo. However flawed, this structure gives continuity and safety that are interpreted as the truth. Of course, much of this tradition was, and is, the truth and ultimately the glory of the Catholic Church, with its claim to be the successor of Christ and the Apostles. But, hidden behind this monumental truth of the Church's uniqueness, is also the fear of change and the distrust and dislike of the spirit of Vatican II that challenges much of this tradition, particularly in sexuality, love and marriage.

Everyone who knows me and reads this book knows my dislike of excessive rules and stress on the law. St Paul realised that the old law was good for conduct but that perfection lies in the new law of Jesus, in the goodness of love referred to in all his Epistles. So I have worked all my adult life to put love at the centre and law at the periphery (realising of course that there must be a minimum of law). I would like to stress that, while the Church should certainly educate for the intellect, it should begin to emphasise in its life, at home and in school, the maturity that is one of the essential foundations of love.

How do we facilitate maturity? The answer is that we are doing it all the time imperceptibly. By highlighting the concept, we can pay special attention to it. In our schools, the process of acquiring knowledge about life, faith and love should encourage reflection, evaluation, discernment, the asking of questions and creativity. We should avoid as far as possible the coercion of fear. In our cognitive development, we should encourage and acquire a sense of fairness, justice, concern and responsibility for our neighbour near and far away. I will deal with developing strong emotional bonds in the next chapter. We are also encouraging maturity in the growth of our faith in schools when we shift from rote learning of the Catechism to an acceptance and appreciation of the Scriptures, our faith and the principles and morality of the Second Vatican Council. Some parents find this threatening and letters appear at regular intervals in the religious journals about the absence of religious education, asking where the Catechism has gone. The Catechism had its uses but we now know that living, serving and loving God, our main aims, are much better served by learning with autonomy, openness and the promotion of living by conscience rather than learning the Catechism by heart.

There is one final point to add about maturity. It is a life-long process and, if post-graduate formation is appropriate for the professions, it is also essential for growth in our faith. There is nothing sadder than the phenomenon I often experience, of listening to highly intelligent Catholics who are brilliant at their work and who remain children in the knowledge and understanding of their faith, embedded in love and its ultimate consummation in the Eucharist. I know that this formation is happening up to a point but it would be even better if we did not consider it only in terms of taking theological courses. What I would like to encourage are courses for personal growth, in particular for marriage, which is the basis and the centre for love in the family. In brief, in addition to the innumerable courses in prayer and meditation currently available, we should be striving to educate people for love in marriage, kinship, friendship, and loving themselves and their neighbours, thus giving people a vision of their vocation and helping them to understand their faith in the context of their ordinary lives.

Chapter 18

Parenting for Maturity

It should be abundantly clear from previous chapters that one of the great revolutions of the last 150 years is a new recognition of and emphasis on something we have always known – that the basis for the adult personality is largely laid down in the first two decades of life, and that parenting in these early years is of paramount importance. This is particularly so in our education for love, the heart and centre of Christianity. The link between love and sex is of special importance because, if we neglect this, we are wasting our time if we try to lay down prohibitions in adolescence. We are also wasting our time if we try to control the emergence of autonomy and its accompanying difficulties in the same period. The responsibility of parents lies much deeper than simply attending to their children's academic education. It also covers human growth, the education of the emotions and the development of individual responsibility. Responsibility is much more than self-discipline. I have seen too many adults who struggle with relational difficulties as a result of being serviced instead of loved: that is to say they were clothed, fed and sent to school and that was all.

The process of acquiring knowledge takes place mainly in schools, but, as all schools realise, this can be facilitated or hampered enormously by the atmosphere at home and the active encouragement of the parents or lack of it. The aftermath of marital breakdown, for example, can have tremendously adverse effects in the home, and these have been extensively studied. Even before a child goes to a nursery, how much time he or she spends talking, reading with and playing with his or her parents is of vital importance. The reading of stories at bed-time or at any time not only enlarges knowledge and imagination, but also has the added advantage of time spent together and the forging of bonds of love. It is also an occasion for providing emotional security and, incrementally, adding to the child's pool of security for life.

Growth of knowledge is not confined to school, but goes on in every area of the child's life as the child relentlessly and persistently asks questions. The child's 'Why?' may stretch the patience of all parents but it is absolutely necessary to respond, and to answer truthfully and not merely for the sake of giving an answer. Truthful answers are one of the foundations of trust for children, although they will sooner or later stumble on the truth anyway. What do parents do when teachers and parents provide two different answers? 'But the teacher says . . .' is a common refrain in many homes. Is either the parent or the teacher a liar? Here it is necessary to introduce as early as possible the reality of the multifaceted face of truth: that there can be more than one explanation. This concept helps the child, when he or she has grown up sufficiently, to appreciate the validity of alternatives and to make up his or her own mind. In the world of morality, it is never too early to teach a child evaluation and the use of conscience. Psychologically, it should be borne in mind that it is not only knowledge that is being offered, but truth, honesty and trust. Children are extremely subtle in testing adults and their contradictions, especially those between parents.

We are all learning that cognitive acquisition of knowledge is influenced by the emotional atmosphere prevailing within the child. Difficulties at home, tension between parents, separation or splitting up may all make attentiveness and concentration at school very difficult. This is not to say that children may not have cognitive difficulties of learning: physical difficulties such as defective hearing or sight, learning problems such as dyslexia and a whole host of other problems may be contributory factors.

It is very common to attribute poor progress in school to laziness, but laziness has innumerable sources. The child may need encouragement, have poor self-esteem, may be anxious and too apprehensive to start a given task, or may be bullied, emotionally distracted and upset, and it is imperative to establish what is going on both at home and at school. Parent-teacher contact is not only an occasion to discuss academic progress but for both to assess each other's personality as well as verifying what the child is saying. Study after study has shown that children may behave one way at home and another way at school. Teachers may and do encourage, but encouragement from parents is of paramount significance and is one way to make children feel loved. That is why it is vital to allocate time at the end of the day to listen to all the details of what has happened.

School is not only about exam results. As children get older, discussion and consultation over choices of subjects to take or drop is very much a parental concern. Above all, the child's education must not be the actualisation of the parents' wishes, the compensation of their own childhood and the fulfilment of their own dreams. The child is a person in their own right as an individual from the very beginning.

When it comes to personal education, parents and the Church have been in the past largely preoccupied with sexual behaviour, moral duty and obedience. But emotions are primarily about love, and love grows in the first intimate relationship of life. I have already mentioned the critical theories of the growth of love. The early years are vital for learning how to be loved, registering love and, in psychological jargon, internalising this love by taking it in and retaining it.

I have already stressed the five elements of this love, namely closeness and availability, both physical and emotional, communication, demonstration of affection, affirmation and resolution of conflict. In the earlier years availability is demonstrated by holding. The nature of this holding can be gentle or tight, suffocating, distant, aloof or warm. There are variations on how we can be held, and this does not entirely depend on the parents but also on the reaction of the child, but they all convey an experience of love or lack of it.

Togetherness is linked with separateness and lays the foundation of the balance between unity and autonomy. Separateness in the early years is often accompanied by the anxiety of separation. The right amount of separation and the balance with closeness are major issues in adult love. The young child has the powerful weapon of crying to bring the parent back when the amount of distance and separateness feel wrong. The right amount of separation is about feeling loved, the wrong amount about feeling abandoned, rejected and insecure, the three enemies of love. These enemies are intimately linked with anxiety and fear. Distance from those we love, if unduly prolonged, produces both anxiety and fear.

Next comes a powerful demonstration of love in kissing, caressing and holding. The commonest way we feel loved and reassured, both as a child and as an adult, is in these ways and they are the most frequent expression of what the young child needs, but touch is important through the whole of life, though as we get older love is expressed at a distance through communication.

The young child loves to be talked to and particularly to be listened to. In the early years the sense of the words means less than a soothing tone. This applies throughout life, particularly when we are feeling hurt: what we hear is important, but even more important is the comforting reassurance of being recognised, wanted and appreciated. The tone of voice makes the difference between feeling ignored, rejected, even marginalised, and feeling understood, acknowledged and having a sense of belonging. As young people, and throughout life, we feel particularly loved when we are affirmed and approved.

All the above expressions of love are important, but verbal affirmation has a unique power that rewards us and boosts our self-esteem. Adults who lack self-esteem, confidence and the assertiveness that goes with it often have parents who never gave much approval and were sometimes actively discouraging: statements such as, 'What do you want to do that for?' and 'You will never be any good at that' are recurring phrases. A correct parental approach is vital, but it must not be forgotten that alongside nurture there is nature: the make-up of the child and its ability to receive and register love. Psychiatry is fond of criticising parents. However, it is the interaction between parent and child that matters and both parent and child can be awkward!

Traditionally in society, and particularly in Christianity, parenting is associated with providing discipline. Many Christian traditions have been preoccupied with the presence of the Devil and sin and the desire to root these out. It makes a great difference whether we see children as intrinsically bad, evil and needing correction and removing from the jaws of the 'evil one' or as basically good but vulnerable because of an initial alienation from God caused by original sin, which can be healed through love.

Needless to say, such attitudes have played vital roles in correction and punishment, and corporal punishment has a long and enduring history in all societies and particularly in Christianity. Its abolition sometimes still elicits die-hard fundamentalist Christian requests for its restoration. Apart from its brutality, corporal punishment has been shown repeatedly by psychology to be a powerful precursor of violence, for those who have been treated violently as children have a tendency to repeat this behaviour. Among the recent scandals that the Catholic Church has had to face, there are many instances of past cruelty in Catholic schools, all delivered in the name of Jesus Christ. Sadly, we wish that such cruelties were not part of the past, and while their prevalence must not be exaggerated, for there was also much loving care, just as in sexual abuse, one case is one too many.

So how is discipline to be enforced, and how do we learn to control our anger and other bad habits? The solution lies in much more than mere control. What we are aiming for is to educate the child to understand that anger, envy, jealousy, hatred and greed not only damage the other person but also ourselves. We damage ourselves by operating on an 'eye for eye' basis, by an absence of care and concern for others, and by building up a bad image of ourselves through loss of control and guilt. The older child can understand all these things when they are explained. The younger child, especially those under five who get in a temper tantrum, needs to be taken away from the scene of the eruption, held safely and strongly until the tears dry up and gently talked to at the appropriate level of their understanding. This is an appropriate method of loving control, and an opportunity for moral principles to be slowly instilled.

In the young child, feeling cut off from the love of the parents and from the paradise of their presence is a profound punishment in itself, and it is absolutely necessary to speed up the process of reconciliation. The young child is repeatedly asked 'What do you say?' and soon learns the response of 'Sorry'. In older children and adults, the sequence of anger, verbal or physical hurt, guilt, apology, reparation and reconciliation establishes a common pattern for dealing with quarrels and conflict. If we believe Melanie Klein, this process starts at around about the sixth month of life.

Conservatives, who love rules, regulations and punishment, say that this is all very well, but children need to know right from wrong. Indeed they do, for no other reason than for their own safety and preservation, but this is not primarily a question of obedience to rules, although this can be necessary for avoiding physical danger, but of understanding how to love ourselves and our neighbours.

The earliest way of encouraging 'correctness' is by introducing a child to the elements of good manners and acceptable behaviour, which is acquired as a conditioned reflex. We start with blind obedience (reflex conditioning), and continue by gradually laying down boundaries of what is permissible and not permissible, once again primarily for children's safety and to develop their love of their neighbours, rather than to enforce our own sense of control. We correct errors in a way the child can understand and respond to, rather than inflicting pain or fear. As I have just said, the most powerful punishment for children is the loss of the love and approval of those they depend upon and love, such as parents, their families, teachers and friends.

Obedience is a favourite word of authoritarians, and in particular of authoritarian Christians, who use Jesus as their principal example. They take the example of the obedience of Jesus to his Father. To interpret the word obedience in an authoritarian sense is to introduce the concept of fear – this cannot have been the basis of the obedience of Jesus, for according to St John:

> In love there is no room for fear,
> but perfect love drives out fear,
> because fear implies punishment
> and no one who is afraid
> has come to perfection in love. (1 John 4:18)

Another reason why the understanding of obedience as a child-like compliance does not apply to Jesus is because of the equality between Father and Son. I am sure that those who see obedience in terms of the fearful compliance to authority so beloved by Christianity will find Greek or other words to support their case. I believe that the real interpretation of Jesus' obedience is commitment based on love. My case rests on understanding human nature: fear is certainly a reason for compliance and obedience, but not an expression of the fullness and highest aspiration of mature love. For me Jesus' obedience, even to death, is an expression of his full and mature commitment to love both for his Father and for the whole world.

Chapter 19

Education for Sexuality

The Church has historically been obsessed with preventing children in adolescence from committing 'fornication' i.e. pre-marital sex. Since young people are now doing this in very large numbers, the Church has become confused and, in the last resort, has turned to rules and prohibitions – the 'Don't do it, it's wrong' mentality. Since this prohibition is usually offered without explanation, the young, who are defiantly claiming the goodness of their bodies and taking possession of them, do not take much notice of this injunction.

The answers to this problem are complex and need to be explored long before adolescence. The basic rule to understand is that what matters is not the individual act but the meaning that sexual intercourse conveys. The heart of any act of sexual intercourse, but in particular pre-marital sexual intercourse, is to link the affection and love learned in the first dozen years of life with the post-pubertal genitality of intercourse. The real heresy of modern sexuality is not primarily that intercourse takes place, but that there is a separation between personal love and genital sex. Both have their own meaning, as I have described when considering sexual intercourse within marriage. The pre-pubertal love is learned in the relationship between child and parents. This love is already 'sexual' in a Freudian sense because of its sensuous connotations of touch, the sensory pleasure of the body and the mucous membrane e.g. the mouth and kissing, and above all the personal meaning of recognition and feeling wanted and appreciated. This 'libido', i.e. love, connects with genital sex.

Pre-marital intercourse was forbidden historically for many reasons, but primarily because of the danger that a resulting child would not be sufficiently cared for. Loss of virginity in the woman would also make her less desirable, lessen her material value, and make her far more difficult to marry off. The woman was considered her father's property: in Deuteronomy we read,

> If a man meets a young virgin who is not betrothed and seizes her, sleeps with her and is caught in the act, her ravisher must give the girl's father fifty silver shekels; since he has exploited her, she must be his wife and, as long as he lives, he may not divorce her. (Deut. 22:28–9)

This Old Testament view of the woman as the property of her family was followed in the New Testament by the Pauline concept of the body as the temple of the Holy Spirit, and gradually a hostility towards sex supervened. With the passage of time, women are no longer seen, at least in the West, as property, and have acquired their own personal dignity in the climate of pre-marital sex. For Christianity the issue should be not 'acts' but the presence and supremacy of love. Every time sexual intercourse is contemplated, the presence of love should be the most important priority. For a long time in Christianity marriage was seen in two ways, as a passport for sexual intercourse and as a source of procreation. As I have mentioned before, until recently i.e. in the last hundred years, and particularly in the Catholic Church before the Second Vatican Council, love played little part in the theology of sex, but now it is seen as having supreme importance in terms of Christian values.

Where is the relevant and living reality of love in adolescent intercourse? First of all, the gap between puberty and marriage may be between 10 and 15 years. Complete sexual abstinence within that time is possible but difficult, to say the least. This difficulty is highlighted by figures for the age of first sexual intercourse. It has been recorded that, amongst women aged 55–59 in the early 1990s, the median age at first intercourse was 21. The age falls progressively to 20, then 19, and for the youngest available cohort, those aged 16–24, first intercourse occurs at 17. A recent study by the Social Exclusion Unit on teenage pregnancy in Britain shows that the number of young people sexually active by the age of 16 doubled between 1965 and 1991, with the rise most striking among girls. It is now estimated that nearly 27 per cent of boys and 18 per cent of girls are sexually active by the age of 16.[1] The most obvious evidence of teenage sexual intercourse is pregnancy and in 1997 in England and Wales 90,000 teenagers became pregnant resulting in 56,000 live births. Nearly 7,700 conceptions were in girls under the age of 16, resulting in 3,700 births.[2]

While there is an increase in sexual intercourse in adolescence, it is not primarily casual. Among those who had sexual intercourse before 16, 35 per cent of men and nearly 60 per cent of women considered themselves to be in a steady relationship. Nevertheless, the study showed that about 25 per cent of men and 60 per cent of women felt they had sexual intercourse too soon and 73 per cent of men and 40 per cent of women considered that they had it at about the right time.[3] The main reasons given for having sexual intercourse under the age of 16 were curiosity in 40 per cent of men and 23 per cent of women, while 6 per cent of men and 40 per cent of women claimed to be in love.[4]

There are, of course, many teenage acts of sexual intercourse that are not motivated by love, but result from psychological pressure, poor self-esteem and a fear of being rejected for social and material reasons. Many young people who feel deprived of love believe that sex will give it to them. Alas it does not, but it shows the link between emotional poverty in the first twelve years of life and adolescent sex.

The influence of parents and the Church in puberty can at least delay sexual intercourse. Clearly the more loving and good the relationship between adolescents, their parents and teachers, the better the prospects of influencing them in this area. The prohibition, the 'You must not', of the Church, has some impact, but this can be very limited. There is a small but fierce argument between those, largely from the secular world, who advocate contraception to safeguard against unwanted pregnancy, and those who want to encourage abstinence, or at least delay sexual intercourse until greater maturity is achieved. I have no hesitation in saying that abstinence until real love enters the equation is both the preferred and the Christian answer.

Sooner or later the teenager will fall in love. We have already looked at the process of falling in love, described by Bowlby as an affective attachment occurring through vision, sound, touch and smell. Adolescents fall in and out of love many times and it should not be presumed that any one occasion is the unique, serious and final defining moment.

How do we recognise when we are truly in love and ready to marry? According to Thatcher,[5] this recognition is vital because our society now allows a pre-conjugal 'betrothal' situation that permits sex, although orthodox Christianity still believes that sex should never occur before marriage. If this rule cannot be accepted, then the serious alternative ethical position is when we are ready to unite personal love with genital expression.

The question of how we make a mature judgement as to whether we are truly in love is the one that schools, parents and the Church should really address, as this is vitally important both for sexual ethics and for the possible prevention of future marital breakdown. The person should start by asking themselves whether they have the necessary loving feelings. The overwhelming majority will say yes. Women in particular will say yes because romance is a very powerful factor for them, and affection and sex go hand in hand for women much more than for men. Far more important is to ask some, if not all, of the following questions:

- Do I want to spend the rest of my life with this person?
- How mature are they? (Maturity here is considered in terms of being reliable and trustworthy.)
- Are they punctual?
- Do they let me down, and if so, how frequently?
- Are they good company?
- Do they meet my needs?
- Is their personality warm, friendly, supportive and comforting in difficult situations or do they run away?
- When I am feeling moody, depressed, sensitive and easily hurt, what is their response? Do they stand by me, withdraw or depart in a hurry?

Research has shown that if people stand by us and are reliable, rather than departing in a hurry, this is a strong indicator of their ability to love. On the other hand, high levels of irritation, anger, conflict, quarrelling and jealousy do not suggest a good future relationship. It is also very important to recognise that existing patterns of excessive alcohol consumption, gambling, drug addiction or a poor work record are not good indicators for a happy relationship, and the hope that 'I will change them afterwards with my love' is particularly dangerous.

I am convinced that addressing these and similar questions are far more important than having classes on the biology of sex and the use of contraceptives. The latter approach fosters not sexual and personal education but an understanding of biology that, although necessary, by itself does very little for the future of personal relationships of love.

If the secular world errs in emphasising biology, Christianity errs in excessive prohibition. What both should aim for is to educate for genuine love. Whatever their background, many young people will proceed to cohabitation, a familiar situation confronting clergy of all denominations. Some clergy refuse to marry cohabitees because they consider pre-marital sexual activity unacceptable, or ask them to live as brother and sister, which I believe to be totally unchristian.

The adverse effects of cohabitation are well and fully described by Thatcher, an Anglican theologian, in his book, *Living Together*.[6] More importantly, he makes a full and detailed case for the Christian legitimacy of what he calls 'pre-conjugal sex' in the presence of betrothal. He wants betrothal restored and he gives a detailed account of it both in the Old and the New Testaments, citing the betrothal of Mary and Joseph as an example. Thatcher makes the case for pre-conjugal intercourse for those who intend to marry.

Much more can be said on this subject, but I cannot emphasise enough that the nurturing of love pre-pubertally is the most effective way of preventing sexual and marital catastrophes. I believe that, if Christianity were to be armed with this approach, it would have a lot to offer to the world, and would be better equipped to challenge the cynicism and hypocrisy about Christian love within society. I am adamant that authentic love is the bridge between Christianity and secular society.

Parents should educate their children for sexuality, not primarily in order to make them avoid sexual acts, but to ensure that intercourse is always set in the context of mature love. This is the best argument against pre-marital sex, for mature love guards against it. Mature love requires the personal qualities I have mentioned here and throughout the book, worked out in an environment of committed, exclusive, faithful relational continuity, reliability and predictability. These are the life-long characteristics that we desire in our hearts, and which define marriage, not as a restrictive institution but as a life-long experience of love.

This scenario contrasts with the use of the word 'love' in disposable, casual, transitory one-night stands, in which intercourse has nothing to do with love but only with the discharge of semen and possibly the presence of an orgasm for the woman. Christianity and parents can educate appropriately by teaching adolescents this distinction and empowering them to take a stand against casual sex, the ephemeral quality of which has been brilliantly captured by the title of the book I previously referred to, *Liquid Love*.[7]

When Christianity can assure the world that it has lost its hostility to sex and has unlearned the word 'No' and substituted the word 'Yes', then the young and the world will listen to and be persuaded by its proclamation of authentic love.

Chapter 20

What Happens When a Marriage Breaks Down?

This chapter will not deal with marital breakdown and divorce in terms of statistics and the impact on spouses and children. There are already a number of books and articles on these topics. I will confine myself to the narrow issue of what happens to Roman Catholics when their marriages break down, and, sadly, break down they do.[1] Such scanty evidence as is available shows that Roman Catholic marriages break down at the same rate as, or perhaps slightly less than, in the rest of society.

How do we identify when love ceases to exist between a couple? What are the main reasons for this and how do couples and the Church handle the situation? There are several ways that marriages end. Occasionally they finish abruptly and one or other of the partners leaves stating, 'I no longer love you.' Psychologically, this means that the attachment or bond that defined the unity of the couple has been eroded to the point of non-existence. For most marriages this process takes years. Another pattern is for one spouse to terminate the marriage because they have had enough of aggression, alcoholism, drug addiction or similar behaviour. Marriages may also end after an affair that cannot be adjusted to or forgiven. It is true that Christian marriage is intended to be for life but, as already mentioned, one priest who has worked extensively in marriage has said, 'Marriage is for better or worse but not for impossible.'

So a proportion of marriages do not survive: love turns to bitterness, anger, and hostility. Marital problems are so numerous and extensive that it is difficult to summarise them. Nevertheless, out of my extensive clinical experience, some patterns begin to emerge. One of the most widespread causes of marital breakdown has its roots in a situation in which, at the time of the marriage, one spouse was emotionally dependent on the other. This dependence expressed itself in leaning on their partner, and expecting their partner to take the initiative for them and to make decisions for them: in other words, to run their lives for them. Such dependent people are usually attracted to and marry a strong, assertive spouse who is happy to take up this responsibility. In due course the dependent person grows, matures and no longer needs the strong, controlling spouse through whom they have survived till now. They become autonomous and independent, and their spouse, who a few years ago was a necessity, now becomes redundant. The usual outcome is they fall out of love with their partner. On the surface, the relationship is apparently unchanged, but underneath, it is profoundly changed and the dominant spouse becomes irrelevant. The emerging partner may have an affair, become more assertive, resist the possessiveness of their spouse, become rebellious and quarrel over details, and there is growing tension. The dependent person becomes a radically different individual and finally departs. Psychologically, it is relatively easy to identify such situations and they should be recognised theologically. Allowance should be made for the personality to emerge emotionally, and it should be recognised that the initial commitment to the marriage was defective and therefore not free.

The next group of problems are more easily recognisable and are caused by addiction or substance abuse, most commonly alcohol. Many marriages break down because one spouse becomes alcoholic, and, despite treatment, cannot give up the addiction. The unreformed alcoholic is a psychologically disabled person who cannot perform their marital duties to their spouse and, in my opinion, the marriage becomes non-existent. This is usually recognised when the drink problem is there from the outset of the marriage, but not so readily when it invades the marriage later. However, the propensity has often been present from the very beginning of the marriage, whatever the timetable. Beyond alcohol, there are hard drugs, which are less common but no less destructive. When established, severe drug addiction is incompatible with marriage. Finally in this category comes addiction to gambling, which can ruin a marriage.

The third category of difficulties are those caused by severe personality disorders. The first group of these are psychopathic disorders. These cannot be clearly or easily defined, but the divorce courts are full of chaotic people who show psychopathic tendencies. These are characterised by an instability that includes an impulsive, unpredictable mood, accompanied by angry outbursts and violence, and followed by regret and profound promises for reform that are not kept for long. Jobs do not last long, there is often deceit in financial and other matters, and, in summary, such people present constant problems and can prove unliveable with.

Under severe psychological disorders, there is a second category, the paranoid personality. Like psychopathic personalities, severe paranoid personalities are rare, but they are equally impossible to live with. People with paranoid tendencies have an irrational belief that people are against them and feel persecuted. This can lead to them becoming very angry and, if provoked, they can cause a great deal of damage.

The partners of people with personality disorders can suffer greatly and over a long period of time. Finally, they give up. In the process of making up their minds to leave, they go through agonies over the apparently immoveable position of the Roman Catholic Church over divorce and remarriage. When an annulment is not obtained, many proceed to second relationships and suffer from a ban on receiving Communion. Their efforts to persevere with loyalty to Christ can be a shining example of faith. Many can tell of amazing hope arising from the ashes of despair, for the Spirit is certainly determined and love can often be triumphant.

When a marriage breaks down, Churches have different solutions. The Greek Orthodox Church allows up to three remarriages and, after much debate, the Anglican Church now allows the remarriage of the divorced in church. The Roman Catholic Church insists that a legal and sexually consummated marriage is for life, and Jesus commanded, 'What God has joined together let no man put asunder' (Matt. 19:6).[3] Much has been written about this subject but at the present the only solution to this situation is annulment.

For many years it has been my conviction that marriage is not essentially a legal contract – this conviction and my thoughts on annulment have arisen from my clinical observations, and I first wrote on this in the *Ampleforth Journal* in 1968 as follows:

> Although men and women can certainly give and receive each other's verbal vows to take each other in marriage, what in fact has to be established is whether they are physically and psychologically capable of effecting a minimum expression of what these vows signify . . . One can say with a degree of certainty that some marriages are not marriages, despite their apparent fulfilment of the usual criteria, because one or both partners are incapable of giving a minimum expression of their commitment to love their spouse.

This view has since prevailed within the Roman Catholic Church and has become the basis for many of the annulments that are now granted by Church Tribunals. Officially, the Code of Canon Law (Canon 10. 95) states that the following are incapable of contracting marriage:

1. Those who lack sufficient use of reason.
2. Those who suffer from a grave lack of discretionary judgement concerning the essential matrimonial rights and obligations to be mutually given and accepted.
3. Those who, because of causes of a psychological nature, are unable to assume the essential obligations of marriage.

The majority of annulments are given for the psychological reasons that I have described. Annulment in the Roman Catholic Church has not had a good press both from Catholics and non-Catholics, but I am a strong defender of its practice when the judges are really well informed about psychology and the nature of marriage.

Some people would prefer the Church to accept automatically Christian remarriage whenever a divorce is obtained. I am against this and therefore oppose both the Greek Orthodox and the latest Anglican positions, because I believe that Christianity should make a very serious attempt to protect Christian marriage and to preserve the pristine standards set by Christ himself. There are few moral prohibitions more sensible than the indissolubility of marriage. One has only to see the damage that indiscriminate and widespread divorce has done to society.

What I strongly object to is the conviction that resort to the law alone is the best way to defend marriage. Readers will by now appreciate that, for me, while law is necessary, it is at the end of the queue in influencing marital behaviour. I believe that the Church must take marriage far more seriously at a pastoral level and understand its contemporary nature in its total complexity. The Church has not begun to understand love from a psychosocial point of view and it needs to do this, and to put into practice the intensive programme intended to prevent marital breakdown that I will outline below.

If marriage is a community of love, the first thing we must do is to pay real attention to fostering the needs of love and nurturing love from the very early years, as I have indicated in previous chapters. If love is the basis of marriage and sex, an appropriate education connecting love and sex should be present from the earliest years. In our schools we should prioritise education for marriage along the lines I have suggested in the chapters on sustaining, healing, growth and sexual intercourse. Neither society nor the Church have yet to appreciate in depth the importance of preparation in childhood for loving personal relationships. Since, as I have said, the measure of a successful marriage has shifted from the integrity of its social roles to the quality of loving relationships, the latter should be central to the thinking of the Church, schools, and the home, with appropriate encyclicals, education for parents and emphasis from the pulpit. There is no excuse for the widespread silence of a positive voice on these matters.

We next move to pre-marital preparation for relationships, love and sex. These are essential, and on the whole, the Catholic Church has a good record on this but a great deal more needs to be done. I have emphasised that marriage is an unfolding journey spanning many decades that the Christian community should be accompanying. How it does this will of course vary, but I suggest two vital ingredients, preventive education and celebration.

Preventive education is eminently possible, but has not yet even been visualised, let alone begun. I have in mind a progressive post-graduate education, by which I mean that the community of the

Church should use the Sacraments to prepare people to anticipate the hurdles of successive stages in married life.

We know, for example, that the birth of the first child is a crucial stage in marriage, and that several challenges can arise to threaten the marriage. The mother may become tired and has less time for the husband who can feel excluded and marginalised, or the mother may suffer from light to severe post-natal depression. For a period of months or even a year, sexual feelings can abate and, if care is not taken, extramarital affairs can result. These difficulties can be anticipated and the complexity of hurt and forgiveness can be discussed within the Sacrament of Reconciliation.

At the time of first Holy Communion, children will have recently entered school and discovered new group dynamics and sources of support. This is a time when they move from the one-to-one unconditional exchange of love within the home into a more competitive academic environment. There is a shift in how self-esteem is acquired as achievement becomes much more significant. This is also a time of enormous busyness for the parents in which the balance between work and home life must be carefully regulated. It is easy for both husband and wife to get submerged in work, children and the pressures of running a home, and an imbalance of all these factors can lead to the danger of making insufficient time for each other.

Confirmation is a time when parents can be given help with the complexity of the process of adolescents separating from parents, acquiring autonomy and yet still needing parental support. It can seem that adolescent children switch instantaneously from being 16 years old to being a toddler! This is also a time when it is important for parents to listen to and understand the emotional and sexual issues facing their adolescent children. From time immemorial, the only concern of Christianity was to forbid fornication. Now there is no excuse for avoiding the complexity of accompanying adolescents in their journey through this decade and the early years of adulthood.

I do not expect priests to do all this, but I do expect them to take this golden sacramental opportunity to assist marriage. A small number of dedicated married people can be involved and, after suitable training with information, talks and discussion, be ready to help couples.

Prevention should be accompanied by celebrating liturgies. Rather than simply celebrating the marriage ceremony itself, the Church should celebrate the whole cycle of sustaining, healing, growth, and sexual intercourse, middle life, the menopause, retirement, and so on: in other words, it should help the couple see Christ in their daily, monthly cyclical life of marriage. If the Church can celebrate the cycle of the liturgical year, it should also celebrate the equally important cycle of marriage.

I believe that the Catholic Church triumphed by recognising marriage as a Sacrament in the Middle Ages. It is the most important Sacrament after Baptism and the Eucharist and the most ignored and neglected. It urgently needs to be put on the map of the life of the Church. The contemporary Western world has never been in greater need of understanding and practising love and entering into and supporting marriage, the cradle of love and sexuality for society. Never before in the history of marriage has it needed more theological and pastoral attention.

Chapter 21

The Family: a Domestic Church

So far a good deal of this book has dealt with marriage and rightly so, not only because I have been studying it for over 40 years, but because I believe that for a variety of reasons it has been grossly neglected by all the Churches, and particularly by the Roman Catholic Church. Some will say that with a celibate clergy this was inevitable, but the Reformed Churches with married clergy have not been much better until the last 50 years or so, and the Second Vatican Council, which was made up of entirely celibate men, brought some brilliant insights to marital love.

Beginning with the Reformation, Luther saw the ends of marriage very much as Augustine and Aquinas did, and took rather a pessimistic view of it as a difficult and unpleasant way of life. Although he was later to marry himself, he believed that, 'according to the Spirit' the Christian had no need of it – it was a disease of the flesh that required it. For him 'shame and nakedness and all things sexual, the burning of lust, the subjection of woman to man, and the pangs of childbirth and the headache of parenthood' were all the result of original sin, and, as we have seen earlier, he referred to marriage as a 'hospital for the sick'.[1] Here the long shadow of Augustine continued. Although ministers were allowed to marry, this was not on the basis that sex was good. As late as 1930, the Church of England decided to permit contraception but did not examine sexuality in any depth. Nowhere did the Reformers link sex primarily with love, the strengthening of relationships and the goodness of sexual pleasure, in a reflection of what Genesis states, namely that everything God created was 'very good' (Gen.1:31). There were exceptions, as there were in the Roman Catholic Church, but by and large until the last 50 years all Christianity followed Augustine in sexual matters.

The link between sex and love in all denominations is about 50 years old and the specific analysis of marital love presented in this book first appeared with the publication of *Marriage, Faith and Love*[2] in 1981. The subject of love and sexuality in the twentieth century is so exhaustive that a whole chapter is devoted to it in my book *Let's Make Love*.[3] For me the saddest part of the story of the theology of sex and marriage initiated at the Second Vatican Council is that it was not pursued because the Church was sidetracked into arguments over contraception. The Anglican Church over the same period has been preoccupied with homosexuality, remarriage of the divorced and women priests, and the issue of homosexuality is now threatening to split the Anglican Communion. As a result, no Church has made a serious effort to transform the insights of this book into liturgies or practices. This is a great pity because God's people, the majority of whom are married, have not connected with God, who is love, in this central aspect of their lives.

What do I mean by liturgies for marriage? I have participated in many such liturgies. Essentially, this celebration is not a Mass but a eulogy to love with texts from Genesis, the Prophets, Tobias, the Song of Songs, the Gospels, Saint John and of course Paul, and other relevant readings. Such readings are accompanied by theological commentaries on love, marriage and sex and appropriate hymns.

A fresh understanding of marriage gives many alternative opportunities for liturgies. Currently marriage is celebrated primarily on the wedding day in all denominations. The reason for this goes back to the Middle Ages, when a feud was raging between those who believed that marriage commenced at the first act of sexual inter-course and those who proposed that the necessary condition for marriage was the mutual consent of the spouses to take each other as husband and wife. Since the Council of Trent, the second view has prevailed and it is the couple who marry each other by the exchange of vows with the priest as a witness. The marriage is ratified by the first act of intercourse, and so the wedding day has come to represent marriage. This view is seriously defective. Marriage is an unfolding journey spanning many decades with a series of crucial events such as the birth of children, all the exchanges of love portrayed in sustaining, healing, growth and sexual intercourse, and turning points such as the menopause, silver and golden anniversaries, retirement and so on. All these could and should be celebrated so that marriage becomes a living celebration of love. This is a richness awaiting all the Churches, whose only real and main contribution so far has been the setting up of Christian schools.

Marriage is a profoundly rich Sacrament for Catholics and a holy estate for Anglicans. The Sacrament mobilises grace but, in my various lectures all over the world, I am still confronted with the idea of this grace seen as a pipeline straight from heaven pumping spiritual energy to the couple.

Since the Second Vatican Council another profoundly rich and infinitely more important concept has arisen:

> For from the wedlock of Christians there comes the family in which new citizens of human society are born. By the grace of the Holy Spirit received in Baptism these are made children of God thus perpetuating the people of God through centuries. The family is, so to speak, the Domestic Church.[4]

This passage undoubtedly emphasises the arrival of children. However, there can be no children without parents who are in a series of relationships of love, extending the essence of the Sacrament as a community of life and love.

The concept of the 'Domestic Church', reiterated by John Paul II in *Familiaris Consortio*[5] offers the whole people of God, particularly spouses and parents, an opportunity to make a unique contribution to authentic theological discernment. John Paul II invites this contribution, saying

> The Church therefore, does not accomplish only (this discernment) through the pastors who teach in the name and with the power of Christ, but also through the laity

and this invitation to married people to contribute to the theology of marriage was often repeated by Cardinal Hume.

In response to this, I have developed in my various writings the concept of the domestic church as the centre of the Sacrament where this community of life and love is situated. This community expresses the Sacramental presence of Christ through every moment of loving encounter of the spouses, and spouses with their children, from making a cup of tea or coffee, cooking a meal, going for a walk, to making love. All these moments of love are an encounter with Christ. When we really appreciate the domestic church as the heart of life and love 24 hours a day, and the communication of grace through these encounters with Christ in and through each other, then the significance of Christian marriage will transform the life of the Church. In these terms, it is a powerful symbol of evangelisation, worthy of constantly being put on the map and celebrated. The domestic church comes particularly alive as living love through sustaining, healing, growth and sexual intercourse.

The Sacraments, including marriage, were instituted by Christ. Though each of them is intrinsically a mystery, they are 'visible' signs or symbols of invisible grace. They are constituted of matter (things) and form (words). They act *ex opere operato*, not by virtue of the personal merits of the minister or recipient. One of the problems of Sacraments that express the love of Christ is discovering and experiencing the mystery of that love through human means of expression and human symbols – bread and wine in the Eucharist, water in Baptism, words in Reconciliation and so on. The people of God have to experience the spiritual reality of the Sacraments by going beyond the human manifestation of the 'matter'. When the bread and wine, for example, are elevated at Mass, we have to 'see' the Body and Blood of Christ. This is an act of faith in which a visible sign or symbol renders invisible grace.

This is the case for marriage, except the ministers are the spouses, and their human acts of love are the symbols of the essence of the Sacrament, their community of love. It is still difficult to recognise the conjunction of human love and the sacramental love of Christ. But with proper education, painfully lacking so far, this is a theology that can be easily understood. The Second Vatican Council defined marriage as a community of life and love, and goes on to say that, 'This love is an eminently human one since it is directed from one person to another by an affection of the will.'[5] So every act of love, not just sexual intercourse, and every encounter with each other can become an encounter with Christ.

Part Four

The Wider Family

Chapter 22

Kinship

After marriage and indeed arising from it, kinship is the next most important and widespread expression of love. Kinship was part of Jesus' experience: 'He was still speaking to the crowds when suddenly his mother and his brothers were standing outside and were anxious to have a word with him' (Matt. 12:46). This is not the place to comment on the actual relationship between Jesus and his family, but this story illustrates that Jesus was part of the emotional world of kinship. Another, and indeed more emotional passage is Mary's visit to her cousin Elisabeth when they were both pregnant (Luke 1:39–45). But Jesus also asks people to leave their family for his sake, although he promises that the family relationships will be restored:

> Peter took this up, 'Look,' he said to [Jesus], 'We have left every-thing and followed you.' Jesus said, 'In truth, I tell you, there is no one who has left house, brothers, sisters, mother, father, children or land for my sake and for the sake of the gospel who will not receive a hundred times as much, houses, brothers, sisters, mothers, children and land . . .' (Mark 10: 28–30)

Sometimes Jesus appears to distance himself from his kin. When Jesus was told that his family wanted to have a word with him, he replied:

> 'Who is my mother? Who are my brothers? Here are my mother and my brothers. Anyone who does the will of my Father in heaven is my brother and sister and mother.' (Matt. 12:48–50)

The point Jesus was making was not the rejection of his human family but the importance of relationships within the Kingdom of

God and with the Father. In John's Gospel, which stresses love above everything, Jesus' love for his mother is shown when he speaks from the cross:

> Seeing his mother and the disciple whom he loved standing near her, Jesus said to his mother, 'Woman, this is your son.' Then to the disciple he said, 'This is your mother.' And from that hour the disciple took her into his home. (John 19:26–7)

This exchange is the first example in the Christian era of the loving and caring responsibility between children and parents that continues to this very day, and the amount of support exchanged between children and parents is generally greater than the amount exchanged between any other kin.[1]

My remarks in this chapter apply only to the intact traditional family in Western society. Other societies have different relationships, and there is extensive literature about kinship in the large re-constituted families that can result from divorce. It is the basic kinship as a form of love that I am emphasising here. I am grateful to my 14-year-old grandson, Luke Milne, for coining the term 'secondary love' for the love exchanged in the kinship of the wider family. It is a very apt phrase, following the primary love of parents and children.

In the wider kinship of siblings, cousins, uncles and aunts, grandparents and other blood connections there are shared values and the provision of role models. Some of the basic exchanges of spouses are also part of the universal characteristics of love in kinship, such as sustaining through availability (depending on geographical proximity), communication (enhanced by the car, telephone and modern technology), demonstration of affection, affirmation and specifically acceptance, resolution of conflict and toleration of differences between kin. Healing is widespread, as kin reveal and share the limitations present in themselves and their relatives, and grow through affirmation and encouragement.

The family in general offers personal, emotional, social and financial support, not only at times of celebration or crisis but also expressed in a continuing conscious awareness of our own identity, of who we are and how we relate. Special mention should be made of the support given to the single person in the network of the extended family. Of course I am naturally stressing the positive, affirmative, loving aspects of family kinship. I am well aware that there are negative features and family feuds are the stuff out of which a good deal of the drama of literature, plays and soap operas is made up.

In the kinship network, siblings play a vital role. Older brothers and sisters care for, relate to and are often delegated responsibility for younger ones depending on gender and birth order. This can lead both to the infighting we are all familiar with, and to moments of endearing exchanges. Sometimes the delegated responsibility can extend to caring for the younger children's basic needs such as food and play, defining acceptable behaviour, making sure destructive play and harm to one's self and others is avoided and entertaining to prevent boredom or restlessness. While all this is going on, the younger siblings are being influenced and learning values, knowledge and skills from the older ones who are taking care of them. The younger ones perceive the older ones as models to imitate, and sometimes the best way to teach is not via parental pressure, but by encouraging younger siblings to imitate their older brothers and sisters, or by simply allowing them to observe them and freely select what they like. This method of learning usually leads to long-term changes in cognitive, emotional and social development. While we learn much from our parents, our brothers and sisters are alternative sources for acquiring knowledge and skills, particularly if the age difference is small and notes can be compared and exchanged.

A study of 39 families in England from early childhood to adolescence found that a warm, fond and supportive relationship with an older brother or sister was connected with better self-confidence and adjustment in the younger child, while negative behaviour from the older sibling was associated with poorer competence and adjustment in the younger. When there was a warm relationship between the siblings, this helped with minor difficulties and major life problems of the younger ones. This study confirms what is well known, namely, when we have a good and loving relationship with our older siblings, this is linked to both temporary and enduring helpful and affiliative support, a natural expression of 'secondary love'.[2]

In our society, mature siblings usually live apart but they remain in touch through visits, outings together, and contact via the telephone or email. Sister-to-sister relationships can be particularly close – our own four daughters go on holidays and outings, shop together and help each other with child minding among many other things. The brother-sister relationship is the next closest, and generally the brother-brother relationship is the least so. Overall, there is a solidity felt between siblings which is expressed in frequent contact, feelings of affection, support at times of crisis and, of course, recurrent family celebrations of special occasions.

As already mentioned, sisters often form the closest ties. Sisters may and do have their arguments, conflicts and jealousies but over time they remain closer and have more affiliative contact than brothers. Sisters, through these closer ties, support each other through every important event in their lives such as marriage, child-bearing (they are often the first to rush to see and hold the new baby), divorce, looking after aged parents, and their own old age and widowhood. Sisters also have a very visible role within the whole family as they tend to coordinate extended family activities and maintain family relationships. For example, one of my daughters specialises in organising the catering for family celebrations. Sisters support their brothers in an affectionate and loving way and these brothers report higher morale and greater feelings of happiness in their life. In short, sisters assume, in our society, a unique and important role throughout their whole life span which is not equalled in the relationship of brothers. They activate and preserve family relationships, care for elderly parents and give emotional support to their brothers later in life.[3] This social and affective support from siblings, and especially from sisters, is the general rule but I am very conscious that not all siblings get on well together.

While it is obvious that parents provide the bulk of support to their children in the first two decades of life, later on it is the children who support their parents. Sociologists estimate that adults may now spend about fifty years relating to their parents. While children usually support their parents at all times, it is of course the needs of ageing parents that are of special interest, and this area has been studied extensively.[4] Both parents and children acknowledge this exchange as a filial responsibility, but how this is executed often depends on the geographical distance between them.

The first characteristic of this filial mutuality is to maintain contact. Then there is the possibility of providing assistance, both practical and financial, if this is necessary and possible. The contact, assistance and communication between children and their parents reflect the need for a balance of closeness and distance, autonomy and dependence, the need to avoid conflict as far as possible, and sharing. All these are felt obligations but, as in all relationships, the need for autonomy and independence are key elements of the parent-child relationship. Thus the elderly often want to stay in their own homes as long as possible and prefer to find alternative solutions rather than going to live with their children, unless there is the possibility of co-existing and yet having separate accommodation. Care of the elderly is much more often provided by women, and although marital partners generally assume the major responsibility for one another in old age, when one of them is no longer able to care, it is often women who provide this help.

A special mention must be made of the role of grandparents. This has been recognised from time immemorial and, in some cultures (for example, in the West Indies) where the father does not always have a big presence, they play a major role in helping to raise the children. In the intact family, grandparents nurture, show affection and express love, although this is often described as 'spoiling'! For the grandchild, their grandparents provide a separate world of love, socialisation, story telling and learning that has a special and enduring place in their lives. Many people whose relationships with their own parents were fragile focus with fondness on their grandparents, and in some instances, children are brought up by their grandparents.

Nowadays grandparents are especially important when both partners are working. They offer support by taking children to and from school and caring for them during the day and in school holidays. Grandparents are responsible for 46 per cent of all child care in Britain, and one fifth of full-time working mothers and nearly a third of part-time ones receive regular help from grandparents.[5]

With the immense increase in divorce, the role of grandparents has become much more significant, but a particularly adverse and sad effect of divorce (among many!) can be the loss of contact between grandparents and their grandchildren. Grandparents are a source not only of personal contact and affection but also of family history, giving their grandchildren a personal account of their lives, which in schools is thought of as social history.

The fun and pleasure of this relationship is a two-way thing. As a psychiatrist, I know a lot of the theory of child development but, when my children were young, I was too busy to observe their lives as much as I would have liked. Now I can observe my grandchildren at leisure, and to my great pleasure can confirm much of the theory I learned and disagree with some of it!

A great deal of what I have described also applies in close families to aunts, uncles and cousins who in addition can provide alternative role models and demonstrate different lifestyles. The love prevailing in kinship, which my grandson called secondary love, belongs to the extended kingdom of love of the family and personal relationships. As far as I know, the Church tends to lump them together as 'family', and there is no formal separate recognition of their role. I have no doubt that kinship, although in a different form, should be included in the life of grace of the domestic church and should be highlighted by the Church, which has massively neglected the total concept of family life.

Chapter 23

Friendship

Commentaries on friendship go back to Homer and many books have been written on the subject. This chapter will not be a treatise on the topic, but will emphasise contemporary adult friendship. While there is an overlap between marriage and friendship, the best declaration of their distinction is the remark often made by spouses, 'My wife/husband is my best friend.' This shows an intuitive awareness that, besides the roles spouses play for each other as husband and wife, there is in addition a distinct relationship of friendship. But, while everyone needs friendship, it comes into its own for single people. Though the concept spans nearly two and a half thousand years and more, and its meaning has changed in different eras, it has always been connected with love and Jesus emphasises this connection in John's Gospel:

> This is my commandment:
> love one another,
> as I have loved you.
> No one can have greater love
> than to lay down his life for his friends.
> You are my friends,
> if you do what I command you.
> I shall no longer call you servants,
> because a servant does not know his master's business;
> I call you friends,
> because I have made known to you
> everything I have learned from my Father. (John 15:12–15).

I shall come back to this link between friendship and love, but in the meantime I want to give a very brief historical outline of friendship. For this I am indebted to Elisabeth Stuart's *Just Good Friends*,[1] which concentrates on homosexual friendship. The commentary on friendship starts with Homer, for whom friendship exists between men of outstanding virtue who hold each other in high esteem and speak favourably about each other. For Homer, friendship is a mutual admiration society. Socrates believed that friendship can exist independently of social status, but relies on shared ideas and feelings. It is a relationship of affinity, reciprocity and mutuality, based on a freedom in which people can discover themselves. Aristotle's writings on friendship were very influential. He described three types of friendship, the first based on utility (people who are useful to us), the second on pleasure (people who are like us) and the third, and for him the rarest and 'purest', based upon character, in which we find a second self. Friends become friends when they admire each other's goodness.

The Middle Ages, in particular between 1120 and 1180, has been termed the age of friendship. Bernard of Clairvaux turned away from the language of war, kings and judges into the language of love, using the Song of Songs as an allegory of Christ's love for his Church. This is of course very different from our contemporary interpretation of the Song of Songs as an expression of sexual feelings. Aelred of Rievaulx wrote a famous treatise on friendship, *De Spirituali Amictia*, based on Cicero's writings on friendship, which he greatly admired. Aelred argued that the whole world was created for friendship and that it can only exist between equals. After the Fall, friendship was corrupted through avarice and envy. Such was the intensity of his belief that he saw friendship in animal life:

> And though in all other respects animals are rated as irrational, yet they imitate man in this regard (friendship), that we almost believe they act with reason. How they run after one another, play with one another, so express and betray their love by sound and movement, so eagerly and happily do they enjoy their mutual company, that they seem to prize nothing else so much as they do whatever pertains to friendship.

Aelred believed that friendship was divine love, and that the Fall had corrupted friendship but after the Last Judgement universal friendship would be restored. He believed that human friendship was the path to friendship with God, and was not afraid of friendship leading to sex, a nightmare of the pre-Vatican II world of religious communities and their concern about 'special friendships'. For him, the physical had a spiritual dimension of love:

> Therefore, in a kiss two breaths meet, are mingled and are united. As a result, a certain sweetness of mind is born, which rouses and binds together the affection of those who embrace.[2]

For Aelred, friendship is a relationship between equals in which:

> Your spirit can rest and you can pour out your soul, delight in their company, can take comfort in the midst of sadness, find peace . . . the (friend) weeps with you in sorrow, rejoices with you in joy, unites with you in doubt . . . Though the body is absent, the spirit is there . . . And you can confer all alone the more secretly, the more delightfully, with whom you can rest, just the two of you, in the sleep of peace, away from the noise of the world, in the embrace of love, in the kiss of unity . . . And unite yourself that you mix soul with soul and the two become one.[3]

Much of this description can be recognised today within heterosexual friendship, but it is not surprising that Aelred is often quoted to illustrate homosexual love.

The sixteenth-century humanist Montaigne regarded friendship as the purest and highest form of love, only available to men. For Kierkegaard, there was, as with Aelred, an innocence of friendship:

> You know how I am, how in conversation with you I jump about stark naked whereas I am enormously calculating with other people. I confide only in you . . . You, my friend, the only one, through whose intercession I endure the world that in so many ways seems unbearable, the only one left when I let doubt and suspicion like a violent storm wash away and destroy all else . . . My Mount Ararat.[4]

Freud had little of importance to say about friendship, but the Object Relations psychologists emphasised its significance for togetherness, love, bonding and attachment. As will be seen, many historical descriptions of friendship, particularly those of Aelred, are immediately recognisable today. This brief historical account of friendship points to the importance previously attached to social status, mental and rational affinities, and, in a hierarchical world, power. In particular for feminist theologians, the subordination of women in marriage is contrasted with the egalitarian quality of modern friendship. In fairness, however, this egalitarian relationship can now also exist between spouses.

The study of contemporary friendship has intimate connections with sociology, but I want to look at the psychological aspects of friendship here. Friendships can range from being superficial and casual across a whole spectrum of depth, intensity and meaning. Sociological research indicates that friendships also differ according to class and gender. Women emphasise its relational aspect whereas men use it to exchange information, enhance business connections and explore professional interests and work opportunities. In other words, women emphasise affection and men functionality. Women in particular discuss matters with their friends which they cannot easily talk about to their husbands.

A stereotype that has emerged from studies of working class communities is that women live in a world of family and kinship and men in a more segregated world of pub, club and trade unions, and, we should add, in Britain, for quite a lot of the year of football. The close mother-daughter bond continues to be of central importance, while the father-son bond is generally considered to be less strong. In particular, men are supposed to lack the capacity to be as expressive about feelings and emotions.

The middle classes have more time, resources, leisure and social skills to facilitate friendship in their lives. Friends are now useful for establishing and affirming social positions, for providing suitable playmates for their children and for sporting activities. It is in this setting that one of the most common social expressions of friendship occurs, namely, entertaining at home and sharing social occasions. One of the most obvious psychological features is that friendship is a voluntary association. There are no rules or legal obligations. Personal choice and selection give it reality, and there are a whole variety of personal friendships based on neighbourhood, work and leisure.

I now turn to the more personal psychological characteristics of friendship. All friendships have something in common, namely companionship and togetherness. It may be remembered that togetherness, communication, demonstration of affection, affirmation and resolution of conflict are central features of marital love. I use the same categories for friendship.

Togetherness or companionship is of fundamental importance because it helps to overcome loneliness. Not only does it help to do this but it also gives an opportunity for communication. Communication can and does affirm the friendship but it is far more important for other reasons. The first and most important of these is that it engenders trust, the key to all intimate relationships. Trust in turn establishes a basis for self-disclosure. This is important because, when we trust our friend, we can reveal a great deal about ourselves. Friends may be more likely to hear the phrase, 'You are the first person I have ever told this.' This disclosure can be comforting, reassuring and guilt-allaying, and can relieve and reduce the pressure of embarrassing secrets. It allows us to talk about parents, siblings, and the memories of early years critical for personal formation. Like marriage, friendship exchanges trivialities but these are the foundations of the continuity of life.

In addition to disclosure, friendship can help us to discover who we are: to reflect on our identity, reveal and affirm it. Self-disclosure can help us to acquire a sense of our continuous and enduring identity. Friends constantly affirm and reaffirm each other and often remove uncertainties about each other. They can spot the gradual and evolving elements of who we are. Meeting again after a while we can say to each other, 'My, you have changed.' 'Really, how? Tell me.' Thus we can discover an emerging unfolding self, which may not be revealed to us through our spouse.

Self-disclosure, however, can be dangerous. We must be careful about the authenticity of our trust in others before revealing our secrets. This is vital because we can self-disclose impulsively as a way of obtaining relief and regret this when we discover that our secret is disseminated and used as blackmail, particularly when the friendship breaks down. It is very important that we do not give hostages to fortune.

Friendship can also be a source of healing. In times of crisis, a friend is someone about whom we can say, 'Thank God you were there.' Millions of telephone calls give this reassurance every day, and what would any of us do without the help of a friendly neighbour in emergencies? More particularly, our friend, like a therapist or a spouse, can uncover our unconscious and help us to see parts of ourselves we are unaware of: 'Really. Am I like that?' However, in using our friends to uncover our unconscious, we must be careful that we do not allow ourselves to be saddled with their projections. The last word must be left to our own discernment and a careful assessment of what we are told about ourselves. External observations are much more likely to be true when they are validated by different sources – there is safety in numbers!

Two of the most common psychological complaints are anxiety and depression. Both can be helped by friends through reassurance and de-conditioning i.e. doing frightening things together. Talking is clearly one of the most helpful aids for mild depression and, if our friends know us well, they will point out the early symptoms of a depression that has descended upon us.

At the heart of a good friendship, as in a good marriage, lie the characteristics of continuity, reliability and predictability. Through friendship we can learn, if necessary for the first time, what love is. We do this by learning that we are lovable, registering and retaining love. In friendship, love is about the sense of belonging, feeling accepted, recognised and appreciated. It is amazing how friends can pick up this relationship as if from yesterday even after years of interruption. Friendship can also have the same sense of commitment.

All this can and does happen without sexual intercourse, although not infrequently lovers can gradually cease to be lovers and become good friends. But sexuality is more than intercourse and friends, particularly passionate friends, can exchange kisses, hugs and rely on touch in the form of embraces to convey their affection and intimacy. The single person need not fear that they are second-class citizens, because they have access to this powerful bond of friendship.

Christianity acknowledges friendship, but, like marriage, it has been seriously neglected theologically in recent times. When was the last time we heard a homily or encyclical devoted entirely to friendship? We have to go back to the Middle Ages to find one of the most comprehensive studies of friendship, one of the most powerful connective links in society. Friendship with God, frequently commented on, must, as love in marriage, be based on the understanding of human friendship, and ultimately it is a powerful way of penetrating the mystery of the Trinity.

Chapter 24

Singleness

Throughout my lecturing career, one of the most common complaints I receive is that I talk about nothing else but marriage. 'What about us?' say the single people. So far I have avoided writing about them because I believe they should describe their own experiences, and because single people cannot be considered as one group, but a whole range of groups. In age order, single people range from adolescents, through the early decades of adult life in which some people would like to marry or form an intimate relationship but are unable for psychological or social reasons to do so (this group is the most problematic and all sorts of dating agencies have sprung up to cater for them). The next category is the separated and divorced, who remain single or reconstruct a new intimate relationship of cohabitation or marriage, and at a later stage, there are the widows and widowers.

Each of these groups has their own characteristics. Of course, there are people who have no desire to marry or to join the priesthood or religious life and are perfectly content to remain single. Equally there are those who are single and unhappy.

Single people who want to marry and cannot do so are the group I am most familiar with because they often seek psychological help. They can be divided into those who have personality problems, and those who reflect sociological conditions: a discrepancy of numbers between the sexes, for example the shortage of men in Britain after the First World War; work difficulties, such as scarcity of land to cultivate; a lack of appropriate social conditions to mix in rural areas, or the need to care for elderly parents.

The possible presence of a personality disorder is a very sensitive

subject, and people can strenuously resist acceptance of this category with the angry retort, 'I am not mad.' Society has seriously failed
to appreciate that people can have a psychological difficulty presenting persistent problems in the formation of an intimate relationship
without being 'mad' at all. We all have a spectrum of difficulties in our
personality from the minute to the severe, which can hinder us from
entering into a close relationship.

Turning to those with difficulties, the first, and in some ways the
commonest, is shyness. There are people who may be utterly comfortable in the familiar setting of work, and intensely shy in a group
or in a one-to-one situation. Some 30–40 per cent of young people
think they are shy.[1] This expresses itself as a lack of self-confidence,
feeling awkward and inhibited, and blushing and sweating on social
occasions. They feel constantly that they have a made a mess of
things, are self-critical and repeatedly say sorry: in other words, they
are continuously apologising for their existence! The first step with
shy people is to reassure them that there is nothing seriously wrong
with them. They should be encouraged to mix, to go out, make
friends, particularly of the opposite sex, and participate in social
gatherings.

These shy, timid people may approach dating agencies and a
certain percentage are successful. What can happen next is that two
timid, shy people form a relationship that, with the encouragement
of friends and the family, advances to the point of going out together.
It can stay this way for a long time and then move on. They may go for
holidays together and talk about sharing the same house, but
procrastinate in doing so. Having negotiated the relationship so far,
they discuss marriage or living together, and once again they delay
the event. Such procrastination may be endless and they may get
stuck at this particular stage. However, they may become engaged
and then, just before the wedding, have an acute anxiety attack,
known as engagement neurosis.[2] Endlessly putting off a marriage,
or cancelling an appointment with the doctor or dentist an hour
before, is a typical behaviour of anxious, shy or timid people, and
procrastination and postponement can become a way of life.

An alternative response to dating agencies is that no one seen is
good enough. Excuses then become a way of life. Some single people,
however, have truly been hurt in a previous encounter and refuse to

be hurt again. If we want to help them, we need to encourage them and endeavour to restore their confidence and trust.

Another personality trait is seen in people with low self-esteem who feel unlovable. They will often say, 'Who would want to marry me?' or, if not actually saying it, think it consciously or unconsciously. They are usually attractive, intelligent and amiable, but their own assessment of themselves is deeply negative. Just as with the timid, they need an enormous amount of loving through persistent encouragement and reassurance. Another expression of this uncertainty is to move from relationship to relationship, never making a formal commitment to anybody or, if a commitment has been made, using any excuse to break it and move on again. At the heart of shyness and low self-esteem is the fear of intimacy. Human closeness engenders social anxiety and sufficient discomfort to necessitate the breaking off of the connection.

Moving onto the more severe and rarer personality disorders, we come to the psychopathic and paranoid people I have already mentioned in the chapter on marital breakdown. Both these severe conditions need professional help. There are also the people who grew up in a home where they witnessed constant aggression, drunkenness, violence or marked unhappiness. These people often remain single because of the fear of repeating these patterns. Nowadays, they may avoid marital commitment and may turn to cohabitation.

Beyond personality disorders, there are some single people who are mentally ill. Easily the commonest category of these are schizophrenics who are actively ill, under treatment, or who are 'burnt out'. These people are solitary, cold, aloof, distant, and find it very difficult to form a relationship. They may be suspicious, feel they are being followed, watched and overheard, and are paranoid.

Schizophrenia is a rare but serious mental illness that needs careful treatment. Even with treatment, the number of schizophrenics who marry or stay married are few. Depression, on the other hand, is very much more common. The depressed are subject to mood swings and periods of moderate to severe depression, when they withdraw into themselves. One of the most serious complications of depression is suicidal attempts, or even suicide. Depressive tendencies do not prevent marriage but, if a depressed person marries a difficult person, recurrent bouts of anger or aggression from their partner or difficulties with in-laws may send them into repeated bouts of depression. Finally, there is homosexuality, definitely not a mental or psychological condition. Tragically, in the past homosexuals may have felt forced to marry from parental pressure or to reassure themselves about their normality.

When we meet a single person in their twenties, thirties, forties or even later, who appears to be anxious, depressed or suffering from poor self-esteem, the best way of loving such a person is to remain close, friendly, supportive and reassuring. The aim is to establish a trusting relationship that will allow them the safety and a stable base to reveal their inner world. Loving them is not advising them, which they may resent, but listening, if necessary for a long time, so that they can relax and regain their self-esteem and their self-confidence. Often single people feel a secret sense of failure. In fact, there is no need for this whatsoever. They have their full dignity as single people, expressed in their work and friendships and in the kinship support that they give, and need to be alive to the fact that God loves them. Single people can also excel with their unique availability and service. Voluntary work is supported extensively by single people, but their free time and availability should not be exploited. Of course, they may see meaning in their life through their service, but they should be appreciated in their own right.

It is catastrophic for a woman who wants to have a child to marry somebody she does not love, or to have a casual affair in order to become pregnant. Children need love from both parents and are not commodities. With the current divorce rate at around 40 per cent, there is a large pool of the separated and divorced who may remain in that state for the rest of their lives, or have an affair, cohabit or remarry. Studies of how various life events cause stress in individuals show that divorce comes second after the death of a spouse, and affects both sexes, although there is evidence that men suffer more than women. The immediate impact of marital breakdown is massive.[3] Divorced people have a higher number of accidents and higher rates of suicide, cancer and premature death. Depression is a very common occurrence in the first year after marital breakdown, and may be accompanied by irritability and an increase in smoking and alcohol consumption. There can be no doubt that both short and long term adverse effects are extensive after marital breakdown.

How can we love the divorced person? As with all single people, we have to befriend them, not taking pity on them, but acknowledging them as people of dignity and worth. Specifically, by being available, we offer a forum in which they can talk about their divorce. They can move from their anger towards the departed spouse to greater serenity and equanimity in which they can evaluate their late marriage and learn lessons from the breakdown as well as facing up to their own responsibility. It is particularly important not to blame the spouse exclusively but to look at themselves, so as not to repeat the same mistakes a second time. We support the divorced through their loss and their accompanying symptoms until they regain the feeling that life continues and has both purpose and meaning for them.

There is one certainty in life and that is death, and bereavement leaves millions of people single. Even though advances in medicine have increased longevity, the inevitable happens sooner or later and is followed by a sequence that is now well understood and to which much loving can be directed. As with love in marriage, there are two stages to mourning, the immediate short term stage, lasting about a year or two, and the long term stage, which continues until the death of the remaining spouse.

We understand much better the immediate aftermath of bereavement through the work of Bowbly[4] and Parkes,[5] both psychiatrists. In the last fifty years, as already referred to, Bowlby formulated the theory of intimate human relationship on the basis of attachment, that is to say that the baby forms an attachment to the mother through vision, sound, touch and smell. Bowlby also observed what happens when the baby is separated from the mother, namely the experiences of anxiety and depression that are described as the grief of this loss.

The link between infantile and adult mourning is that both are responses to loss. The process of separation, divorce and bereavement can all be seen as having similarities with the experiences of young children between the ages of six months and three years when they are separated from key figures in their lives. This makes psychological sense, as all are mourning experiences. The pattern of this has been described in terms of protest, despair and detachment. As far as the young child is concerned, one is familiar with the picture of the toddler waking up in the cot, standing up, holding the bars of the cot and scanning the room for its mother, not seeing her, continuing to search and then beginning to cry. This is the protest phase. Crying usually brings the mother, but if the mother or a significant figure remains absent for a long time e.g. for several weeks, the child begins to despair and become withdrawn, not wanting to play and uninterested in toys or things. After some time, the child becomes emotionally detached: that is to say, it actually loses its bond with the mother.

A few people have noticed the same processes in marital breakdown. Spouses protest this time not when their spouse is away, but when they are in conflict with one another, or when they don't speak to one another for days. If their relationship does not improve, there comes a longer period, covering perhaps a period of years, when they endure their problems and, finally, lose hope that things will change. At this point, they may withdraw emotionally from the relationship: as the young child gradually detaches itself from mother, spouses simply detach themselves from each other. This is the phase when they come to counselling, but usually it is too late. They articulate the simple sentence of emotional cut-off: 'I no longer love my husband/wife.' To an experienced counsellor, this is a signal of irretrievable breakdown.

The finality of marital breakdown is also seen in the death of the spouse or friend. The first reaction to death is a stunning degree of numbness. This is a feeling which comes within a few seconds and may last for hours or days: 'It doesn't seem real. I couldn't take it all in. It doesn't register.'

After this numbness, fear and alarm follow, just like the child who loses sight and contact of its mother. A couple who are close experience the death of their partner at this stage as an alarm reaction, described as a pang of grief, consisting of irritability, anxiety and psychological pain. This feeling may show itself as 'being on edge', snappy, irritable or easily frightened. The most common symptom is the loss of, or difficulty in getting off to, sleep.

Intimately related to this alarm reaction is that of anger and irritation, which is equivalent to the child's protest. No amount of anger will bring the dead person back, but it is there, and is commented on by many widows. This anger arises from the feeling of being abandoned, a feeling which is aptly described as, 'Why did you have to do this to me?' This anger cannot be easily directed against the dead person, but onto others, such as employers, 'They killed him', or to those last in attendance, such as doctors, nurses, hospitals or ambulance drivers. There are those, of course, who recognise that no one is to blame, turn their anger inwardly and become depressed. They blame themselves for nagging, ignoring the deceased's needs, or not noticing early warning signs and not calling the doctor soon enough.

The immediate seeking of comfort is an expression, like that of the young child, of searching. The search may be conscious, prolonged, and deliberate. 'I can't help looking for him everywhere, Doctor. I walk round searching for him.' The young baby clinging to the cot similarly searches intensely, with their gaze fixed on the door waiting for the mother to reappear. The dead spouse is 'seen' in the street, in the car, in a familiar chair, in bed. Widows can experience hallucinations, or have a sense of their spouse's presence.

The whole sequence of the Crucifixion, Resurrection and Ascension, and Thomas's desire to touch and put his fingers in Christ's wounds, reminds us how crucial it is to differentiate between authentic resurrection and hallucinatory appearances. With the passage of time, the process of searching recedes, and it is sometimes replaced by an encounter with the beloved: not a physical encounter, but rather an awareness of the internalised sense of the spouse, a sense of closeness in which it feels as if the deceased is inside us.

Then, as the child loses its emotional attachment, so the bereaved goes through a process of detachment, and slowly, over a year or more, the period of severe grief is over. But relationships that have lasted a long time leave their imprint, and become part of the survivor, and the memory of the dead survives the sorrow of the mourning process. Mourning has a depressive quality, but this is precisely as it should be. It is the exception for the depression to become so severe that treatment is needed.

The bereaved not only go through psychological changes, but also face social ones. He or she, particularly she, can be left without financial, housing or other social support. This is particularly difficult when the house is part and parcel of the husband's job. People come to the funeral and then forget the mourning person. Returning to and succeeding in life as a single person may present difficulties. A couple is an acceptable and easily integrated entity in social life. But the widowed have no clear-cut role and present problems. None of these is insurmountable, but their resolution involves the presence of an enormous amount of love, to offer succour and to overcome the difficulties that people experience towards the widow whose grief and status make them feel uncomfortable. Having given the customary and acceptable condolences, how does one continue to comfort: in other words, love further? It is this uncertainty, rather than deliberate rejection, which makes the plight of the widowed, in particular, more difficult than it need be. In fact, the isolation and social devaluation of the widowed have been recognised by many religions, and an ancient solution was the Hindu tradition of Suttee, with the wife going with her husband into the funeral pyre.

Love of the bereaved requires a less barbaric answer. The network of kin, when it exists, provides companionship and support. But if all of us can love the widowed by keeping our homes open, inviting them to meals, going for holidays with them, or more simply by inviting them to social and personal home events, then we can make a loving difference.

The widowed, depending on their age, apart from turning to their friends, may remarry, cohabit, come closer to their children, develop new interests or hobbies, join clubs and groups, or do further study. The widowed are one of the largest segments of single people and they need all the love we can offer. This can be expressed not by taking pity on them or being condescending, but by genuinely appreciating their dignity and worth. Other cultures more readily appreciate the elderly and the single person who is widowed. From the Cross Jesus asked John to take his mother into the bosom of his family. We must take the widowed into the bosom of our family and into the community of the parish.

I want now to comment on three issues that particularly involve the single person: temporary sexual relationships, the difference between loneliness and aloneness and envy.

It is commonly believed that a single person cannot live without sex. This is a myth. There are priests and religious who have a perfectly contented nature and a creative life without genital sex. It must be remembered that the recent sexual scandals in the Catholic Church involve a minute proportion of its members. There are many single people who are not in religious life who do not have sex. This is not to say that they may not be under pressure to have it but, for a variety of reasons, they resist.

The myth is that sex is necessary for the single person for their physical and mental health. It is not. Many people will find this statement staggering, given how much sex single people have. It is true that there are biological pressures that demand a release of sexual tension. But, if it is only these pressures that need releasing, masturbation would be resorted to as a relief, and sometimes it is. The real answer is that sex is an encounter with another human being. Fairbairn, the Object Relations psychologist, maintained strongly that the human condition is primarily person not libidinal seeking – we simply need contact with another human being and very often the hidden agenda of sexual intercourse is just that.

So-called promiscuity is not primarily a hunger for sex but a hunger for a person and, if possible, for love. The promiscuous person is often someone who is very needy for love, but finds it difficult to believe that they are lovable, and finds it even more difficult to register and retain love when it is offered. This is one of the least appreciated patterns of human behaviour and it gives us the chance, in the presence of such a person, not to criticise or condemn, but to identify their need for love and offer it in the form of persistent friendship.

When we meet a single person in any of the situations described so far, we inwardly ask the question of how they cope with their single state. There are many very happy single people. Many are contented in the peace of their aloneness. Contented aloneness is a state when the person is in touch with their inner world, has a high sense of self-esteem and creativity, and is at peace with themselves. This may take time, struggle and prayer to achieve. However, some single people are very lonely and long for friendship, and may turn to sex, drink, gambling or superficial socialising to relieve their loneliness. Once again our availability in terms of friendship is our demonstration of love. This availability can be emotionally expensive. We may have to listen to the same story many times, to the same minute and trivial details of their life experiences, to sacrifice our free time, our desire to do the 'this' we want rather than the 'that' with them that they desire. Like all friendship, it carries its own cost.

Many people at times have wished to become a couple, to have children, and to enjoy the life and company of being a twosome. All these aspirations are realistic and understandable. A few, very few, however, move from these natural wishes and are unconsciously envious of their contented twosome friends. This envy is sometimes coupled with bitterness, anger and resentment, and may show itself in a variety of ways. From the length of this chapter and the subjects covered, all of which deserve and have had books written about them, we can see how varied the single state can be. It is my justification for avoiding tackling it for a long time and I am conscious that this present contribution cannot do justice to the breadth of the subject in any way.

Chapter 25

Religious Life

In the aftermath of the Second Vatican Council, there was a mass exodus of priests and religious from the Church. Rome insisted on some assessment of their mental health, in the belief that they might be mentally ill, before they could be laicised. Since there were few Roman Catholic psychiatrists in Britain, I had the privilege of seeing nearly two hundred priests and religious at that time and since, and gained a very extensive insight into religious life in communities.

Firstly I would like to consider the motivation for entering the priesthood or religious life. It is clear that, from the 1950s until the present day, the official, conscious, recognised motive for entering was the presence of a religious vocation, the desire to be close to God and to be dedicated to serving him, just as in marriage, the conscious motivation is to marry the person with whom you have fallen in love. But in both states there are unconscious motives which we are only now beginning to appreciate.

The vocation to the priesthood or to the religious life is an expression of a desire to embrace a life shaped by spiritual growth through regular prayer, liturgy, participation in the Sacraments and work. However, hidden within these vocations were often a number of unconscious issues that are now recognised. The first was immaturity. Under the guise of protecting men from the temptations of the world, potential vocations were often identified in junior seminaries and then transferred to the senior ones. From an early age, boys were incarcerated in an environment that fostered infantility, immaturity, dependence and an ignorance of how to be human. The same applied to women who, at the 'appropriate' age, which could have been as early as 16, entered their convent. The baggage both priests and religious carried with them is the same as for those who married young; that is, with the passage of time, they matured and fell 'out of love'. They entered religious life immature, that is to say child-like and dependent on the authoritarian life of the Church and their communities. When they too gained their confidence and no longer needed to lean on figures of authority, they left and they left in droves. This was nothing to do with mental illness, but had its roots in the collective naivety of the institutional Church in selecting immature people.

Another unconscious reason for choosing the religious life, connected with the first, was fear. Many of these priests and religious were really scared to live with the responsibilities of adult life. They were totally dependent on the system of the wider authoritarian Church and their institutional life within the seminary, monastery or convent. Once again, when they matured, they no longer needed the protection of their environment. Also, in the prevailing atmosphere of the Church then, and in many ways now, their sexual ignorance was nearly total. Some of them, through a natural growing in maturity, became aware of their sexual feelings and, often after agonising, left and married.

In certain cultures (for example, in Ireland), a vocation was a cultural, not a personal choice and was often heavily influenced by the mother. Nowadays, when education, autonomy, and personal choice are operating, vocations have dwindled and one bishop in Ireland said recently that he will not now ordain another priest during his term of office because no one had entered the seminary. A similar situation is prevailing in Britain, but the bishops are not facing up to reality, and persist in keeping the remaining seminaries open. These continue to attract conservative candidates whose desire for the old clerical dress, the Latin Mass and similar liturgical support symbols hides their insecurity. Priesthood and the religious life can also be a place of retreat for the homosexual, not that mature homosexuals cannot have a genuine vocation and be marvellous priests.[1]

Another motivation towards the priesthood and religious life was the advantage of higher education for the poor. When we hear of the numerous vocations in the third world, there is always the possibility that the Spirit is truly calling people in these places, but there is also the possibility that this is a search for free education. In one institution I know and lecture to, a high rate of overseas candidates for the priesthood leave after completing their education and before entering the priesthood.

Genuine vocations will return when their source, the family, is really understood in its modern form by the Church, and promoted by the implementation of Vatican II teaching. When Council's ideals of freedom of conscience, maturity and responsibility are realised, then the priesthood will be seen as a genuine and attractive service of love, not a refuge from sex and the world.

Nevertheless, the single person in the priesthood and religious life continues to be a personal channel of Christ's love. It is hard to exaggerate what the Church and civilisation owe to this generosity of love. Through monasteries, wisdom, literature and art were preserved in the Dark Ages. Scholarship in monasteries was a prelude to the flowering of the universities where religious became eminent teachers. Beyond education, hospitality was another sign of the monastery and convent and, in the days of old, pilgrims and travellers needing food and shelter found them there.

In our own age, Catholics and others owe a great deal to the sisters and brothers who have offered their whole lives to the education of children. It is fashionable nowadays to criticise this education and to highlight unacceptable patterns of discipline and sexual abuse, but we must not forget the sheer effort and dedication of many. Certainly sexual education was pathetic, but this was, and is, a problem of the whole Church and society. Beyond education, sisters and brothers excelled in the area of the care of the sick and nursing. They offered a service that ultimately saw the patient as another Christ and went beyond the technicalities to love the whole person. They looked after the elderly long before it was fashionable for the secular world to do so. They also cared for the poor and the handicapped. In the midst of the current crisis in religious life, these glories spanning centuries must not be forgotten.

There are also the enclosed orders where daily prayer and worship continue. These beacons of prayer are vital for the life of the Church and for the rest of society. Most religious take the three vows of obedience, chastity and poverty. Here, as in the rest of the Church, the renewal suggested by the Second Vatican Council and respect for the advances in understanding contemporary human beings and in psychology must replace some aspects of a tradition which has many good points, but also a deeply flawed understanding of issues such as that of sexuality and authority.

Starting with the vow of obedience, the superior in the community is there to organise (assisted by a council), preserve and serve the life of the community. Obedience in religious life has a further dimension. It is a special recognition of authority. It should not be a power struggle with superiority and inferiority at stake, or an expression of child-like dependence. The religious person has every right to think for themselves, and to express those thoughts in their regular gatherings.

Chastity is not a vow to deny the sexual part of the personality – this attitude and the accompanying ignorance of the past have no place in contemporary religious life. Religious are sexual people as much as anybody else. The vow is to express sexuality not as genital sex, but as sublimated into love.

The heart of poverty is not the lack of possessions, but the meaning we invest in them. Possessions are there to be used and appreciated. They are not there to give us our sense of identity. As Christians, we are not to live by kind permission of our possessions. The Kingdom of God and God himself are the ultimate criteria by which we live. Obedience, chastity and poverty are not just rules for religious. They are, properly understood and maturely exercised, the framework of life for every Christian.

But how is this to be achieved? In the Church in which I grew up, reason and the will were the key instruments of growth towards sanctity and maturity. Deprivation and asceticism were believed to be crucial for sanctity. Psychology teaches us that, while reason and will are important, so are emotions, and that even more important are the principles of sustaining, healing and growth, in and through love. Wherever I lecture on these principles, religious agree that they apply as much to their lives as to the married. What differentiates them is genitality and children.

Another feature of the pre-Vatican II Church was that the Magisterium, namely the Pope, the bishops and the priests, were the most significant part of the Church and the laity were there very much to listen and obey – in some ways they were considered to be spiritual second-class citizens. This was not an attitude of arrogance on anybody's part, rather it was accepted as the sacred order and structure of the Church. With the Second Vatican Council came a revolution in thinking about the laity. The sacredness, dignity and responsibility of the lay person was spelt out as never before (those who want to verify this statement need only to read the Council's statement about the lay person).

The spiritual superiority accorded to the single state has also lasted all my lifetime and is only beginning to fade now. This is a curious interpretation, given the fact that married people make up nearly 90 per cent of the Church. The poverty with which marriage has been treated is not only an appalling neglect of the majority of the people of God, but, as I have written extensively in *Let's Make Love*[2] and in this book, is based on a deeply flawed sexual theology, spanning 2000 years, with a lofty view of virginity.

Whatever my and many other people's reservations are, and they are many, about John Paul II, he has been a generous recorder of the importance of marriage and of sexuality. He has given this Sacrament high praise in his encyclical, *Familiaris Consortio*,[3] where he speaks of marriage as the primordial Sacrament.

Nevertheless, I must finish this chapter with a critical evaluation of the single state dedicated to God, and a comparison of it with marriage. The Pope himself says:

> Virginity or celibacy, by liberating the human heart in a unique way, so as to burn with greater love for God and all humanity, bears witness that the Kingdom of God and his justice is that pearl of great price which is preferred to every other value no matter how great, and hence must be sought as the only definitive value. It is for this reason that the Church, throughout its history, has always defended the superiority of this charism to that of marriage, by reason of the holy singular link which it has with the Kingdom of God.

John Paul II cannot be criticised for writing this. He is only repeating what the Church's tradition has always asserted. I would nevertheless assert that tradition has grown up side by side with a flawed theology of sexuality which, until recently, has ignored its intimate connection with love and spiritual grace. The fact that the Second Vatican Council has defined marriage as a community of life and love, combined with its thinking on the domestic church and the theology of personal love in marriage, allows the couple to encounter Christ from moment to moment in their everyday life. The single person's availability for service is beginning to be matched, when properly examined, by the availability of the married to Christ through each other and their children. This is a continuous encounter with God, who is love. There is nothing inferior about this life of grace. In the light of these observations, I would ask whether the traditional thinking on the superiority of the single state dedicated to God will stand the test of time, in the face of this unfolding theology of marriage.

Chapter 26

Work

In the whole of my life I have rarely, if ever, heard a sermon wholly devoted to work. Yet for most men and women, their sense of self, their identity and their image of God are based on work and their home. The neglect of this subject is a very good example of the present disconnection between the institutional Church and the laity, the lay-religious divide and the conviction that spirituality and contact with God largely depends on how much time we spend in church. This conviction is quite different from my view that the Christian life should be seen as a daily encounter with Christ, spanning home and work.

Since I claim no special expertise on the subject of work, my background reading comes from two different sources. The first is John Paul II's encyclical, *Laborem Exercens*.[1] He has unique experience as a worker and this encyclical shows his usual brilliancy, although some would struggle with his philosophical, theological and phenomenological approach. As with all his encyclicals, this one presents the reader with the formidable and daunting task of interpretation, but, unlike the encyclical on marriage which is theoretically based, this one has the distinctive advantage that he has had the experience of being a worker, although, of course, not living a life combining work and married home life.

Another source I have used is *Thank God It's Monday*[2] by Mark Greene, an Anglican from an evangelical theological background. Clearly Greene's approach is a contrasting one to that of John Paul II, but both emphasise the importance of work as an encounter with Christ and its importance for evangelisation. I have read both sources and have used my own psychological experience to formulate some thoughts on work which focus on its personal aspects, rather than on economics, the organisation of capital and management.

John Paul II insists that work is rooted in the theology of the Bible. He refers to Genesis.

> God created man in the image of himself.
> In the image of God he created him,
> male and female he created them.
> God blessed them, saying to them, Be fruitful, multiply, fill the earth and subdue it. (Gen. 1:27–28)

Here the implications are that we are created in the image of God in many senses. The one I have chosen to emphasise in this book is that we are created to love and that is our principal feature, but in the above passage we imitate God as creatures furthering creation. So when we are in the secular workplace, we are in the presence of God, cooperating and extending his holy work. We are thus engaged in a spiritual, divine dimension. John Paul II stresses the creativity and dominion we express in human labour. For him it is a fundamental dimension of man's existence on earth. Through work, people draw close to God, participating in Christ's threefold mission as priest, prophet and king. As one might expect, given his concern about human rights, he sees work as an expression of man's dignity, and throughout the encyclical he refers to just rights, fair conditions, and the place of the trade unions.

Work is not only associated with human dignity but with fulfilment, what could be called self-esteem in psychological terms. John Paul II here uses an interesting and innovative phrase, suggesting that Genesis is the first 'Gospel of work'. This Gospel is continued in the New Testament, emphasising that Christ too was a worker. The Kingdom of God was entrusted in the hands of somebody who had been a worker and who chose workers as his apostles.

> With the coming of the Sabbath, he began teaching in the synagogue, and most of them were astonished when they heard him. They said, 'Where did the man get all this? What is this wisdom that has been granted him, and these miracles that are worked through him? This is the carpenter, surely, the son of Mary, the brother of James and Joset and Jude and Simon? His

sisters, too, are they not here with us?' and they would not accept him. (Mark 6:2–3)

This passage emphasises Jesus' link with work. His work was both manual labour and the establishment of the Kingdom of God. His uniqueness was to combine the manual and the spiritual and integrate them. This is our task, to combine our work and at the same time express it as divine implementation of the holy.

John Paul II concludes with the biblical reference to God's work and rest pattern, something very applicable to human life. He underlines that one of the important aspects of work is the advance of science and technology, vital tools for Western society and ultimately for the whole world, the value of work in the development of personal and professional skills and, of course, in the context of a global economy, productivity and profit.

Some Christians feel ambivalent about profit, seeing money in negative terms as the work of Mammon. It is nothing of the sort. Jesus told the parable of the talents, which is the story of the man who summoned his servants and entrusted his property to them, giving to one five talents, to a second two, and to a third one, each according to his gifts. He praised the men with five and two talents who traded and doubled the amount, but reprimanded severely the third man who buried his one talent to keep it safe (Matt. 25:14–30).

For me, this parable not only supports the concept of responsible financial speculation and the taking of risks for profit, but it is also a parable for the Church, which has to choose between burying its talents by being safe and conservative, or advancing the Kingdom of God, in and through love, by being bold and taking risks as the Second Vatican Council did. The New Testament is clear that the Kingdom of God is not about fear but trust in God in and through love.

There are manuals galore about the organisation and administration of work, an area that is not my expertise. What I do know is that the best theoretical plans fail if the human factors, i.e. the relational aspects of work and the psychological elements governing the employer/employee relationship, are not given serious consideration. Here, as everywhere in Western society, we are moving from an authoritarian boss/worker relationship to one of increasing egalitarianism, where employees and those in the lower echelons are seen as people of dignity, where consultation is highly prized, and where attitudes to authority are moving away from fear and pseudo-respect, to the desire to be consulted, kept informed and taken seriously. A world that is growing aware of this democratic structure finds the hierarchical, non-consultative, authoritarian approach of the institutional Church difficult to accept.

The best organisational structures in contemporary work assert the importance of fairness, justice and the avoidance of exploitation. The personal assessment of individuals in a firm in which the management gives its opinion and the workers see the report and respond is in marked contrast to the secrecy of the institutional Church. Many business people have commented to me that the institutional Church would not survive very long as a business concern. To which the Magisterium, or at least some of the Magisterium, would reply, 'But the Church is not a business.' This, of course, is not true – its outer institutional framework is a business running its inner sacred world, the Sacrament of Christ and, because of the way it is behaving, millions are leaving it.

Some moral theologians have concentrated totally on business ethics. Once again I do not consider myself an expert in this area and so my remarks here are generalisations. Clearly business and work should adhere to the Ten Commandments with respect for truth, honesty, integrity, and giving value for wages and salaries received. Being in the presence of God minute by minute in the workplace, in the same way as at home, in a constant encounter with Christ in relationships, means that every minute of work should have a God-awareness, and be filled with God's values of honesty towards the task performed.

Morality goes hand in hand with the task of developing, through the minutiae of work, one's own identity. John Paul II separates the objective content of work and the subjective aspects of the worker. Psychologically, there is the objective side e.g. writing a proposal, putting columns of figures together, working professionally as a doctor, lawyer, judge etc., and the subjective side, the relational aspects of the work. As a doctor, indeed as any professional, the quality of the relationship, for example with patients, and the quality of any service, be it manual labour or professional, should be an engagement with others and a labour of love. In the process of living with our colleagues, clients, patients we are constantly discovering who we are. Our mistakes and crises are all opportunities to learn, and this is expressed in this book as a loving labour of sustaining, healing and growth-promoting.

These aspects expressed in relational terms have two features, namely how we treat ourselves and how we treat others, particularly our subordinates. Do we understand our own identity? And do we love our fellow workers? In a different age we would talk about the 'character' we possess, and people are constantly assessing each other's 'character' in terms of the trust we can offer.

Another significant psychological issue is that of ambition. Ambition is, of course, a powerful and very important human characteristic particularly applicable to work. My professional life, however, has taught me to be very careful about this word. There are those who are never satisfied. An exaggerated example of immature ambition is the scientist who gets one Nobel Prize and then wants another. Never being satisfied is a psychological problem.

Where do human satisfaction, fulfilment and happiness begin and end? This is a very relevant issue both in work and at home. Is our identity defined by our possessions and status – our home, our car, our wealth and our position at work – or an inner sense of fulfilment, peace and joy? Something that concerns everybody, but particularly Christians, and has a special application to work, is how we acquire a sense of ourselves and self-esteem. This should not be primarily through our possessions or status, but through our inner contact with, communication with and awareness of Christ, and through a vision of work as divine creativity present in loving relationships.

Just as within human relationships we must grow in autonomy, not living by kind permission of others, so in work we must mature in loving ourselves and learn to live without the power of money, possessions and status. The socialist ethos and its political implica-tions may reply, 'That's all very well, if first you have enough possessions to survive,' and it is true that we all need a certain amount of money and possessions to reach a minimum standard of living in dignity.

The problem here is that affluence is relative. When is enough enough? I have already referred to the psychologist Winnicott, who, faced with a world of mothers concerned as to whether or not they were adequate mothers, tried to reassure them with the term 'the "good enough" mother'. 'Good enough' was his ultimate motto. A key to satisfaction in work and in life is to aspire to perfection, but to be able to live at peace with a 'good enough' position, in which status and possessions fulfil the requirements of our dignity without becoming our ultimate goals. This enables us to avoid pursuing these goals for their own intrinsic worth, and to resist feelings of failure if we are not able to achieve them.

We are here to use the material world without becoming identified with it. We know that it is wrong to exploit anybody, and particularly the vulnerable, but what we are not so clear about is exploiting ourselves through setting unrealistic standards that we cannot achieve. It is clear that Jesus' authority depended on his inner certainty of who he was, what he had to do, and what he had to achieve, and so he could speak with amazing authority and from the Cross say, 'It is accomplished.' Ambition can be a positive force, but restless ambition is a problem, and Christianity has not paid anything like enough attention to the psychology of the person of Jesus, which can show us how to be fully human at work.

An important aspect of work is how it can affect health. Companies have now realised that stress is an important factor which can damage production and profit, and have introduced medical and counselling services. But there is also a great need for private, interpersonal healing and loving. Greene says:

> Britain's workplaces, and this also applies to other parts of the world, are filled with all kinds of people with all kinds of problems such as illness, fear of redundancy, adultery, grief, confusion, purposelessness, ethical conundrums, criminal negligence, racism, dirty tricks and so on.[3]

Some of these problems are dealt with in codes of conduct, particularly in sexual matters, discipline when rules on timekeeping, drinking etc. are broken and, if necessary, tribunals for unfair dismissal and discrimination. What I have in mind is something quite different. What happens, if someone, for example a colleague, approaches you with a marital problem, or concerns or worries of a personal nature? You may want to escape as soon as possible, or feel you should offer advice, but think 'What do I know about it?', and both these reactions are understandable.

The organisation[4] that I set up in 1971 for marital research and practical work for the prevention of marital breakdown faces similar problems with, for example, health visitors and general practitioners, who often see marital problems and face two realistic difficulties; firstly, that they too know very little about marital issues, and secondly that they do not have the time to get involved. One Plus One developed an approach called Brief Encounters that has proved very popular with all professionals, but especially health visitors, and I feel that some of the concepts used in Brief Encounters also have a wider application in responding to work colleagues who come to you with some difficulty. I stress 'come' because heaven forbid that we become busybodies, using the knowledge we acquire through gossip to offer unsolicited advice. What Brief Encounters provides is the reassurance and confidence not to run away or to take evasive action when we are approached. It does not assume any expert knowledge, although in the case of marital problems the course gives some help with them. The course has been the brilliant work of Dr. Deidre Morrow whose genius I here acknowledge with thanks, and what follows is a brief outline of the crucial points.

First of all, we need to be alert as to how these problems may manifest themselves in our colleagues or neighbour. They may be withdrawn, weepy, agitated, or just say, 'I feel dreadful.' You can encourage someone by creating an atmosphere of relaxed welcome ('Sit down, you look worried') and by assuring them of confidentiality ('It won't go beyond us'). The scene is now set for the first step, namely to acknowledge and engage with the person.

The next step is an invitation, 'Would you like to talk?' Many people do not realise how healing talking is. If they do talk, the listening must be empathetic: that is, careful and interested in the content and the feelings expressed. If they take up the offer, be enormously patient: do not interrupt except for clarification, give time for the whole story to unfold, do not take sides, do not be judgemental, and above all do not give advice. Don't say, 'If I were you, I would do this or that' – you are not the other person. You are there to offer time and, in the old-fashioned phrase, 'a sympathetic ear'.

If you do not have the time there and then, arrange for a time when you are free and also for a confidential situation. It is amazing what a little time can do to relieve the stress, share the problem, release anger and reduce anxiety. The revelation and the talk, can be as little as five minutes long, with the promise, if needed, of a longer period later. All that matters is that a moment of confiding has been created. You can finish by saying, 'I would love to hear how things work out.'

What appears here as an absurdly simplistic encounter of healing is in fact an opportunity to love someone through concerned listening, and through offering the opportunity for a trusting sharing. Being a confidante offers hope, even if you have not offered any expertise. What has been achieved is that a new beginning has been established – a space and a loving moment have been offered in the relentless, anonymous and busy world of work.

Clearly confidentiality must be preserved. Do not go home and recount the story, however tempted you may be. You never know who your spouse knows, and what connections, inferences or influences might be at work.

Here I am stressing the loving and healing possibilities of listening. The Brief Encounter moment not only applies to tangled human situations – all workers are subject to worry, problems of trust, anxiety and insecurity in and about their work. Many of us may already have applied the principles of listening and sharing in our workplaces, but we need to appreciate that this is a real loving Christian response to the very common reaction, 'Why bother? There is nothing to be done. It's not my problem.' Everyone is our neighbour.

John Paul II refers to the connection between work and the family. Living this connection can be very stressful. There is a biblical awareness of toil in work and, of course, this can have a huge impact on the family. The first and obvious purpose of work is to earn enough resources to maintain the family, but a workaholic of either sex can be a threat to a marriage and a family if both spouses are so tired that they do not want to make love, or if a working spouse comes home late and does not see the children. Both can also bring the problems of work home and unload on each other, not as a narrative, but expecting solutions, and if depressed, they will bring their depression home with all its adverse consequences.

Unemployment can also have a shattering effect on the family.

Money is a complex phenomenon. Most people ask the simple question, 'Is there enough?', but money has an emotional meaning as a symbol of love in the attitude: 'If you loved me you would not keep me short', 'If you loved me you would buy this or that for me.' A common source of marital conflict is that the wife feels that her husband does not want her but her body, and the husband feels that his wife does not want him but his money. He may try harder and harder to buy love, not realising that love cannot be bought.

Nowadays both spouses often work, and there is the challenge for both, but particularly the wife, to reconcile the demands of home and work. It is still not widely appreciated that it is she who has both to work and carry the major responsibility of the children and the home. This can cause tiredness and reduce the time spent with children. Society does not appreciate the importance of parents spending time with their children and spouses with one another, and so family life is damaged for the sake of profit.

The subject of work is extensive and I have done little justice to it here, but I conclude by reiterating that while working, we are in the presence of God. Work is an extension of God's loving creativity which we can all share in, and we should not underestimate its importance because our identity depends on the living connection of work and home. Work is a source of pleasure, achievement, toil and stress, and so, in combination with marriage and the family, it is part of the domestic church.

Finally, I would like to give a loving acknowledgement of my wife and her hard work, and of all women who keep the homes of Western society going. My wife's complaint is that, while others can retire, she never gets the chance!

Chapter 27

Loving Ourselves and Our Neighbours

'Master, which is the greatest commandment of the Law?' Jesus said to him, 'You must love the Lord your God with all your heart, with all your soul and with all your mind. This is the greatest and the first commandment. The second resembles it: You must love your neighbour as yourself. On these two commandments hang the whole Law, and the Prophets too.' (Matt. 22:36–40)

In a book dedicated to love, we have to concentrate on these words of Jesus. I will start with loving ourselves, for the simple reason that our ability to love our neighbour ultimately depends on how loveable we feel about ourselves. We cannot give what we do not possess, and we give in proportion to the love we feel for ourselves.

I will begin with Freud, Jung and the concept of maturation. Freud concentrated on the first half of life and Jung on the second, and maturation is a process throughout life. A simple definition of loving ourselves is as looking after ourselves, taking care of our bodies and minds and avoiding stress as much as possible. Everybody can agree with this simple principle of self-preservation and of being kind to ourselves.

At the root of loving ourselves lies the problem of selfishness, which casts its shadow over the whole of society and Christianity. It is so easy to fall into the trap of thinking about love of self in these terms, and there is a conspiracy that starts very early on in our lives to make sure we remain humble. Parents and figures of authority fear that we will exaggerate our worth and ego and become arrogant. The real danger is not that we will become big-headed, but that we will lack confidence and self-esteem. In truth, we can compensate for lack of self-worth by exaggerating our capacities and appearing to act arrogantly. How do we build confidence and self-esteem? The key to loving ourselves is twofold: firstly we need to 'possess ourselves', and secondly we need to feel good about what we possess. This is a psychological definition of love of self.

We start possessing ourselves in childhood by all the ways I have already described in Object Relations theories, namely, by taking in such qualities as the loving touch of our mothers, reliable and predictable feeding, sleeping, playing, and rejoicing. In the first stages of babyhood we should feel that our body is good and loveable, that we own it and that we use it as a means of loving others through vision, sound, and touch. This is how the ability to relate lovingly is established. The key to this loving possession, now and throughout our childhood is affirmation, and we learn approval through phrases such as 'I like the way you did that.' Empowering, enabling and constant loving appreciation helps us to learn to possess and we learn not only to possess but also to feel good about ourselves.

As we grow we are gradually separating from our parents, and by the time we are two or three we have learned to walk, talk, dress and feed ourselves. This enormous acquisition of skills extends our autonomy and continues to give us our sense of being good and loveable. Freud writes about the personality developing on the twin instincts of sexuality and of aggression but the later Object Relations psychologists extended this concept to the quality of the interaction between these instincts and the loving quality of parenting. Sexuality in these early years is not the genital form with which we are familiar but the sensuous interaction with parents that, in the presence of their love, makes us feel good about our bodies and loveable. Dealing with aggression is a matter of handling screaming, temper tantrums and so on, which requires the parent to hold the child as securely and lovingly as possible until the agitation settles, avoiding the child feeling bad about its rage, while constantly setting limits and boundaries.

Learning to possess our bodies in an affirmative way is the key to these early stages of growing. By the age of two or three, the child will feel safe to leave the intimacy of the parents, and particularly the mother, for short periods, as the child will have learned to derive security from keeping her presence in the psyche during the mother's physical absence. At about this time or even earlier, the child acquires the emotions of envy and jealousy. Envy is an experience of wanting what another possesses: in this particular case what the mother possesses, or, as the child begins to play with other children, their own toys. For a child, envy is normal, in that it feels small, helpless and inadequate and wants to possess all the resources of their parents and other children. But as he or she grows older, this feeling recedes as the child acquires most of the characteristics that the adult has and there is no inequality left. In wounded people, the remnants of envy may continue into adult life.

Jealousy is the move from a twosome to a threesome, as we experience competition between ourselves and third parties. For Freud, this is crucial in the resolution of the Oedipus complex. Triangular situations are constantly occurring in life and have to be resolved. Both envy and jealousy are threats to love of self. In the one case we want to acquire by any means something we feel we do not have and long for, and in the other, we fear the loss of something, usually someone we love, to a third party.

At the age of four or five we start school, and the process of cognitive growth which has already begun begins to have a more formal framework. Our self-esteem begins to be linked with status, peer relationships and intellectual achievements. Then comes puberty, with the incest taboo and the growing sense in adolescence that we now possess a sexually attractive body, a cognitive mind and an integrated personality. We begin to feel loveable enough to seek and be worthy of the affection of another person. The acquisition of selfhood in the course of development is part of what I mean by possession of ourselves and feeling good about what we possess. We can summarise the first two decades of life as laying the foundations of feeling loveable. By the end of the second decade we have separated almost completely from our parents and are ready to bring the love of our first intimate relationship to the next loving intimate relationship. For the overwhelming majority this will express itself in cohabitation and then marriage, but it is also expressed in our relationships of kinship and friendship. It goes without saying that this loving growth within ourselves is physical, emotional, social and cognitive.

Jung was an early pupil of Freud but then these two giants of dynamic psychology quarrelled and separated. Jung is a complex and difficult psychologist to understand and what follows is a mere outline of his theories rather than a comprehensive and detailed account. Freud was an atheist, but Jung was not and considered religion as an essential natural and legitimate dimension of the psyche, in which God and therefore love existed. For those who want a fuller account of Freud, Jung and religion, see *Freud and Jung on Religion*.[1]

Like Freud, Jung believed in a personal unconscious but he also believed, far more fundamentally, in a collective unconscious. The collective unconscious contained the accumulated inheritance of our race and is expressed in the psyche in what Jung called archetypes. These are primordial images which recur in myths, legends and fairy tales, and which constitute elements of the unconscious. They are normal and universal, and the unconscious organises them into our conscious ideas. While theoretically there is no limit to their number, practically some are more important than others. The first is the Persona, meaning originally a mask worn by actors to indicate a role they played. Psychologically, this is the outward social expression of our personality. In our Persona we play a part that for Winnicott is the distinction between the false and the real self. In contrast to the Persona, the Shadow is the archetype that designates that part of ourselves we do not wish to reveal at all. It is the part of ourselves that we do not want to display, and includes inferior character traits and other unacceptable tendencies.

Beyond the Persona and the Shadow, there is the Anima and the Animus, the feminine and the masculine aspects of ourselves. The woman has to incorporate her masculine side and the man his feminine side. In very simple ordinary terms, growth of love of self is the gradual integration, with growing confidence, of the Persona with the Shadow, and of the opposite side of our sexuality into our personality.

According to Jung, the integration of these and other archetypes leads to the sense of Self as a sense of wholeness: in Christian terms, holiness, and love of self. Jung believed that we integrate the conscious and the unconscious parts of our personality through the process of 'individuation'. This is really the process of integration of our personal life of childhood with the various archetypes into the whole of Self, resulting in a harmony between the self, society and the world. For Jung, individuation is coming to 'selfhood'. It is the culmination of childhood in adulthood, the pinnacle of Self, in which we relate to ourselves, to others and to God. It is a process of lifetime development, leading to a mature self. Some consider individuation Jung's finest contribution to psychology and, in terms of this section on love of self, the Self of course reflects God.

Freud gave us the patterns of love laid down in childhood and the processes of healing in interpersonal relationships, and Jung the hope and possibility of further development in adulthood. These processes are helped by psychoanalysis, but are universal possibilities for all of us without it. I have tried to describe this in my psychological study of Jesus.[2] It is essentially what we find in Jesus, a fullness of Self, capped by the complete confidence of self-esteem, availability and the giving of himself to the whole world and for all time. It is this psychological wholeness that allowed him to speak with the convincing authority which amazed the crowds. It is this inherent authority that allowed him to set the Kingdom of God in motion.

Between Freud and Jung, we have a basis for understanding love of self. But this love of self must ultimately be embedded in our nature, in our infrastructure. As I have mentioned previously, since the time of the Greeks we have put the intellect and intellectual ability on a pedestal. The intellect, with its capacities for abstract, analytical, logical, sequential and predictive thought, is the focus in our schools and universities, but not the goal of wholeness that Jesus taught us to aspire to.

Briefly, the personality is made up of the body, the intellect, and the social and emotional dynamic attributes described throughout this book. In addition to all this, Piaget and Kohlberg added the sense of justice, rules, and fairness. We reach maturity when all the constituent parts of our physical, intellectual, cognitive, emotional, social and spiritual being have developed to their full potential, and we possess them in a loving acceptance of ourselves and a readiness to give to our neighbour. This process is, of course, a lifetime task as we are all climbing this ladder. What stage we have reached varies in all of us and in various stages of our lives.

In a Christian sense, everyone is our neighbour. The lawyer who was keen to justify himself said to Jesus, 'And who is my neighbour?' (Luke 10:29). Jesus' answer, in the parable of the Good Samaritan, has reverberated throughout the world to this very day. Having dealt with marriage, friendship, kinship and work, here I am addressing the question of loving both the visible people present in our lives, and our invisible neighbours far way. We love materially, socially, educationally, emotionally and spiritually.

In advanced Western societies, dire material poverty is not common, but it still exists and we see the poor as beggars in the street, as asylum seekers, in orphanages and in institutions abroad. We put our hands in our pockets and we give money. We may even work personally in various overseas projects. In previous ages, poverty was to be seen everywhere. There is still intense poverty in some third world countries, and in the Catholic community the aid organisation CAFOD does splendid work raising millions annually.

We should remember that our nearest neighbour is the old man or lady next door who we shop for, take to hospital or church and keep company with. Serving on local councils or doing voluntary work are acts of love for our neighbour. Some of this mundane love goes unnoticed. I am always struck by love on the road from the driver who lets me out of a side turning, or stops and lets me pass in a difficult situation. It is the small things that show love. Nurturing our children and helping them to develop their intellect through school work, reading and writing, are all works of love. The authentic teacher teaches because they love children, and we all remember what we owe to a particular teacher.

Emotional love is, of course, the most important and difficult. I have referred to it throughout the book and I will simply summarise its qualities here. First is empathetic, non-judgemental, affirmative listening, giving careful attention to the signals given by our neighbour and picking up both the rational and emotional content of their communication. We should avoid giving advice as much as we can, however tempted we are. Avoid saying, 'If I were you I would say or do this or that' – the fact is we are not our neighbour. Listening in itself is loving. We should try to help the other person reach their own solutions. In order to love, trust is vital and we should pay particular attention to confidentiality and avoid gossip.

Beyond listening, there is, of course, forgiveness and healing. I will finish this section on loving our neighbours with a detailed psychological examination of trying to love the neighbour who finds it difficult to be loved. Everyone recognises and occasionally finds it difficult to love the people who struggle to register, retain and feel our love. This affects many people, and being loved can be a nightmare for some people.

We can start by recognising the fact that, according to Fairbairn, we are not primarily seeking to make sensual or libidinal connections. On the contrary, we are born for contact with others: we are 'person orientated', and our most basic need is the love of others. But the hurdles to receiving it can be myriad, and include deficient parenting and the vicissitudes of life. The wounds of feeling unloved are present to a variable degree in all our neighbours throughout our lives, and the principal challenge for all Christians is to recognise and to respond to them. I know that God loves each and every one of us: after we transgressed at the Fall, he sent his Son to reconcile us to him, and loves us afresh with even greater intensity. But if this truth is not to stay an abstract, intellectual, philosophical notion, then our interpersonal love must be the first human basis for recognising and receiving God's love.

There are a number of stages of loving our neighbour, in particular the neighbour who is wounded, as we all are, and who finds it difficult to be loved, and these are as follows:

1. Don't impose love. So many loving people are frustrated and disappointed because they try to love and are rebuffed. We must be patient, have our antennae continuously open, and read the signs of need carefully: these can include agitation; the shadow of depression and anxiety; worry; confusion; perplexity; asking for advice; telling a tale of woe; trying to ingratiate themselves; clinginess and so on. We know how and when to pat a dog or stroke a cat. We have to learn to recognise and appreciate the signals of love sent out by humans. The mother knows how to love her baby because the baby's signals are there in abundance. We have to recognise the hurt person and the signals they give.

2. Appreciate Freud's concept of defence mechanisms. These are psychological behaviours that we use to protect ourselves from the pain and anxiety of our hurts. In the case of those who feel

unloved, one of the commonest defences is to pretend that they do not need love, that they are self-sufficient and can do without it. As we approach them, they show every sign of this defence. They withdraw, and repeatedly remark, 'I'm all right', or if they are angry, 'I don't need your help', 'I don't need charity', or simply 'I don't need you.' They go to extraordinary lengths to show their independence by hard work, staying aloof, struggling with their difficulties, going on holidays alone and so on. The lesson here is that if you sense the person's needs and requirements for love, to avoid at all costs being put off. Loving needs a great deal of patience. This is what God has shown us, the patience of waiting, watching, and never being put off. In addition we need to encourage and appreciate their achievements and wait for the next move.

3. Create an atmosphere of confidentiality and trust. If they take the first tentative step to reveal part of themselves, we need to listen with immense attention, and if possible to make the time to listen. One of the roots of feeling unloveable is that in the past parents in particular, but others in general, never had enough time for us. Listen carefully and, if you are short of time, ensure that another meeting is arranged.

4. If childhood trauma is revealed, be sympathetic but do not criticise the parents. It would appear that this is precisely what your neighbour wants: confirmation of their anger. Corroboration of hurt is important but collusion with vilification should be avoided. Despite all appearances to the contrary, people want to feel that their parents loved them, and at whatever stage of life they are, they want reconciliation.

5. Don't fall into the trap of believing an idealised picture or retrospective interpretation of family life. When hurt, we do not want to admit that our parents were less than perfect. Only time and confidence will allow the trauma to be revealed. This may be the continuous absence of love, approval or acceptance, a preference for a sibling, a lack of affirmation, or feeling wanted only when appearing clever and achieving academic results: in other words, not feeling loved for oneself.

6. If revelations are made, what Freud called transference may operate, in that your neighbour may project on you their

experience of their parents. In particular, if you say something wrong or make a mistake, they are liable to say, 'You are just like my mother or father. What a fool I have been to expect anything different.' Do not get upset, angry or irritated. Do not show it even if you are, as you are likely to be. Gently point out that you are not the parent, that you are you. It is very common to see a parent in a close friend. Do not try to be technical or psychological or use psychological jargon. You are likely to be met with, 'You too are trying to fob me off with psychological jargon. I do not want to be treated like a case. I am a person.' Do not make the mistake of getting technical even if you are trained, just remain a friend.

7. Lack of love is intimately mixed up with anger. Do not be surprised that, at the point when you feel you are getting somewhere, there is an outburst of anger. Do not feel 'This is the thanks I get for trying to care and love.' This is a way of testing how far they can go in provoking you and still retain your love. Be prepared for angry retorts like, 'You just don't understand, nobody understands.'

8. When you are succeeding and your neighbour really begins to feel loved, they may take a turn for the worse and become depressed. The fact is that they have been familiar for such a long time, ever since their childhood, with the feeling of being unloved: when that changes, it is a new experience that they have to learn from scratch. In the course of learning there is an interval when they may feel like an orphan. They do not know who they are and whether their new loving feelings will stand the test of time. They are terrified of losing what they have gained, so their reaction may be, 'I wish I had never started this . . . I wish you had left me as I was.' Be prepared for this no man's land state and be patient. Learning to be loved is like learning a new language.

9. Loving another person takes time. Even when success appears through a growing sense of trust, feeling comfortable, mutuality and contentment, it can take a long time to consolidate these gains, perhaps years. Do not get fed up. Remember how long it took for the hurt to become established. Do not expect quick fixes. After all, how many broken covenants did God have to overcome to continue with his love? Above all, be patient with the repetition of their stories.

10. Be careful with the use of touch. If the friendship is between a

man and a woman, touch can be misinterpreted as a sexual advance. Even touch as a hug and embrace needs caution and the right circumstances, and should only take place after having spent some time establishing trust.

Needless to say these phases apply to all intimate relationships, are not sequential, and sometimes you may have to retrace your steps, but through them anxiety, aloofness, fear can gradually be reduced.

I have taken a great deal of space to describe loving a person who feels unloveable. I have used an example familiar through my counseling work, but these ten steps apply to all of us, as we are all in various degrees and states of feeling unloved and unwanted. What we are aiming for is to hold people's hands while they find their feet to walk, and to pick them up repeatedly when they stumble. That is God's way of loving.

In terms of spirituality, everything I have written in the third and fourth parts of this book is spiritual loving, because for me love is the essence of offering God through ourselves to our neighbour. But a special form of loving spirituality is constant prayer. By this I mean awareness of God despite lack of concentration, interruptions, and all the familiar distractions. Prayer is a constant readiness to encounter God, not only with words but in a beautiful moment of nature, a scene, hearing a piece of music, or anything that raises our recognition of our immanent awareness of the transcendental 'other'. Spiritual love is constantly seeing in our neighbour the God we love, and loving them.

Chapter 28

Two Churches: the Domestic and the Local

In chapter 21 I quoted from the Second Vatican Council on the concept of the domestic church:

> For from the wedlock of Christians, there comes the family in which new citizens of human society are born. By the grace of the Holy Spirit received in Baptism, these are made children of God, thus perpetuating the people through the centuries. The family is so to speak, the Domestic Church.[1]

I pointed out that the reference clearly applies to procreation but, since children need the love of their parents, the words 'domestic church' apply to the whole family and the relationships within it.

In this chapter I want to take this idea further. In the first part of the book I wrote about the decline in church attendance in the last few decades, the disconnection between the Church and the life of ordinary people, and the difficulties of thinking that we can only connect with God in the sacramental life held in the building of the church. To counter this, I visualise a dialogue, a tangible connection, between the domestic church of marriage and the local church, celebrating the Sacraments in the parish church, particularly the Eucharist. The grace and life of prayer through the love in the family, present throughout the week in the domestic church and the daily encounter with Christ, should be brought on Sunday to the Eucharist, and the graces of the Eucharist should be carried back to support the domestic church during the week. The connection, of course, is the presence of love in the two Sacraments, two holy experiences regularly meeting each other.

This theological proposition means that the Christian is in the presence of a continuous encounter with Christ in a life of love. The secular-spiritual divide and the Sunday-weekday divide of being in the presence of God largely for an hour each week (except for daily Mass attenders), will be overcome. What is more, these two most important Sacraments will be brought together.

If this theology is acceptable, it means firstly that marriage, as defined in the Second Vatican Council as a community of life and love, will have to be put on the map. It will have to receive infinitely greater attention from the bishops and the clergy and from lay people. It will take time to see the importance of marriage and the domestic church in the life and prayer of Christians. Prayer as a communication with God will be present in each and every moment of the spouses' encounter with each other and their children in and through love, and these encounters will be sacramentally one with Christ. Such a view of marriage will have parallels with the monastery in its round-the-clock praise and encounter with God.

Secondly, in order to achieve this vision, we will have to go further and see the Sacrament of marriage not only in terms of the wedding day, to which it has been largely confined for historical reasons, but also as an unfolding journey spanning many decades. This is the second theological point that has to be put on the map.

Thirdly, there are practical implications for this vision. Everyone working in this field acknowledges that, while education for marriage initiates the spiritual preparation for this Sacrament, there is an urgent need for education and support throughout the whole life of the marriage. The Church has previously accompanied the married and the family primarily through its schools. This is not enough, and it certainly does not prevent marital breakdown. At present there is no spiritual formation of marriage continuing after the wedding day. I would like to suggest that two or three lay people help with the continuous formation of marriage at the various Sacraments of Baptism, Reconciliation, First Communion and Confirmation, by preparing the couple to understand how their married life will unfold, and its impact on them and their children. We also need to support marriages between these sacramental moments by regular celebration of the constituents of married life in church and home.

To sum up, all I have said is intended to announce a vision of an intimate and continuous exchange between the origin of grace in the Sacrament of Marriage and the golden riches of two thousand years of liturgy and Sacraments in the Church. This model will offer a concrete opportunity to involve lay people in the continuous round-the-clock prayer of their actual married life, to connect their Sacrament of Marriage with the Eucharist, and to give the laity a proper formal spiritual dimension. The success of such a model, of course, depends on its theological integrity, its acceptance, adoption and promotion by the Church, the stressing and preaching of it by the bishops and the generosity of the clerical world who might feel, but definitely will not be, ousted from their exclusive spiritual position, power and status within the Church. It also depends on a theological advance in appreciating the communion between the spouses and their children, as a powerful channel of grace and prayer that supplements other forms of traditional prayer.

I now move to a fuller extension of the idea of love within the domestic church. I have been aware for a long time of the importance of the 'secondary' loving forces of kinship and friendship and their connection with the home and the family. The Church has an official status for the priest, bishops and the Pope, and for married people in general, but no specific way of acknowledging kinship and friendship, both of which, but particularly friendship, played such an important part in the life of Jesus. I propose that kinship and friendship be included under the umbrella of an extended domestic church on the basis that both are pivotally dependent on the relationships of love that form their basis. This 'communio' is the life of the Trinity and deserves a spiritual acknowledgement, given all its implications for love. I have not outlined this proposal before and, of course, it needs theological consideration.

Extending further the concept of the domestic church, I propose that work, a vital contribution to our identity, should also be considered under this umbrella. Of course, work may have its own spiritual status and that needs further examination. Finally, the single person should also be considered as part of the domestic church, although this is more complex as there are many different expressions of singleness, from the adolescent to the bereaved.

What I am suggesting is that the lay person, so long out in the spiritual cold, be gradually integrated in a theological structure with its own unique spiritual patterns of prayer in and through love and spiritual celebrations. The lay person has been marginalised in the world of the Church for too long, with spiritual status attached to the clerical vocation. The Second Vatican Council indicated strongly that everyone is part of the people of God and, through their Baptism, shares the prophetic, priestly and kingly vocation that Christ holds. All this might appear to threaten the spiritual status of the priest's unique sacred office. The importance of the priest is not based, however, on power but on loving service of love, and is linked with all the other vocations I have mentioned.

In the spirit of this book, all relationships of love reflect the Trinitarian relationships of love and, although a hierarchical church such as the Roman Catholic Church may see this is as the beginning of the lay person intruding into the uniqueness of the priesthood, I see no danger of this, for I do not see the people of God as fighting a power struggle. Everyone has their gifts and spiritual vocation and Paul outlined these different gifts repeatedly. I am suggesting that everyone should be working together for the Kingdom of God. There can be no doubt that the fullness of grace is expressed round the Eucharistic table. Equally, there can be no doubt that the Church has been very much the poorer for ignoring the riches of loving relationships, reflecting the 'communio' of the Trinity in marriage, kinship, friendship, singleness and work. My hope is that this chapter will inaugurate much theological thought to which both the single and the married will contribute.

Chapter 29

Psychology as the Handmaid of Theology

In this short chapter, I want to make a plea that psychology is formally made a handmaid of theology and stands on equal terms side by side with philosophy. In its present form, it has been with us for nearly a hundred and twenty years, beginning with Freud's work, and has transformed Western civilisation. It has been frequently referred to in the Second Vatican Council and by John Paul II, and has entered everyday life and ordinary language. It is imperative for interpersonal relationships because of its understanding of the dynamic concepts of the unconscious and the Freudian and Jungian theories of the personality. In particular, the concepts of defences and transference are extraordinarily useful in understanding human behaviour, and especially sin and moral responsibility.

I do not want to be misinterpreted as suggesting that psychology has eliminated personal freedom, choice, and the concept of sin through determinism, but there can be no question that our picture of human responsibility has been completely changed through recognising and making allowances for both conscious and unconscious motivation. This dimension is already operating in moral theology and in society in our developing understanding of responsibility, justice and punishment. Psychology has dramatically changed our understanding of the operation of human relationships: this is its age and I contend that it has already made, and will continue to make, a large contribution to our understanding of the world in general and the Trinity in particular, given that this is based

195

on relationships of love and the balance between separateness and oneness, fusion and singlehood, all expressed through love.

Psychology's contribution to understanding love, the heart of Christianity, is unique, as this book has tried to show. We know that we can love more fully through better communication, through understanding conflict and its resolution, through guilt and forgiveness and through growth and healing, and thus bring the understanding of the Cross nearer to us. Psychology can help us to understand selfishness and distinguish it from narcissism and the lack of self-esteem, and, as I have shown in the chapter on loving our neighbour, is helping us with this most difficult art of loving. I have tried to describe this love in marriage, kinship, friendship, singleness and work. Psychology has also helped us to make huge strides in understanding marital breakdown, and indeed any fracture of an intimate relationship of love.

By exploring infancy and childhood in detail, psychology has clarified the foundations of love and its maintenance throughout life in and through relationships. As I have tried to show in my book on the psychology of Jesus, psychology is essential in approaching and trying to understand both the unique mystery of incarnational love and his amazing authority. Understanding, or getting near to understanding, Jesus is essential if we are to live Christ-like lives.

A short course or brief introduction to counselling would be invaluable for the training of priests, religious and indeed for everyone working pastorally. I know that in many places, particularly in North America, this is already in place in the education of priests, religious and pastorally orientated lay people. I want to extend this and to suggest that in the United Kingdom the nearly empty seminaries should be used for psychological training. I am not saying that psychology will stop us being selfish, stop us sinning, or stop the fracturing of relationships but it already helps enormously both with healing and with the prevention of trouble.

I know I am biased against philosophy (I freely admit that), and yet I am fascinated by it and my library is stacked with philosophical works. Nevertheless, I find it an exaggerated cerebral occupation in which philosophers often seem to be talking exclusively to one another. It could be argued that psychologists do the same, but psychology has infiltrated society through literature, theatre and films in a way which philosophy rarely does. No one can deny the place of philosophy but now, at the stage humanity has reached, I would insist that the combination of an acquaintance with the framework of psychology, some awareness of the principles of counselling, and Christian compassion and care is the best approach for a whole range of human problems. These include relational difficulties, marital problems, depression, anxiety, the early stages of mental illnesses, personal predicaments such as separation and divorce and issues such as alcoholism, gambling and attempted suicide, but this approach also has a wider relevance for industrial relations and ultimately the whole of society.

I am not advocating that the clergy become psychiatrists or psychotherapists, although some do, but simply that they are trained to pick up and deal with elementary problems and common difficulties, cope with them as best as they can and, if necessary, direct people to experts. Most human problems are relational difficulties with loving. Of course, social issues such as money or the lack of it, housing, and the stress of maintaining a home can all be problematic, but relationships of love are at the heart of human happiness. They are, after all, the key to the life of the Trinity, and I believe that anything that helps us to get closer to that mystery is just as vital as anything we have in our current spiritual life and theology. If anybody says there is not enough time in the seminary to expand on the subject of psychology, let us curtail a little the time we allocate to philosophy (*pace* philosophers).

Chapter 30

Evangelisation and Living Love

In an attempt to address the perilous levels of church participation in Western society, there have been concerted efforts in evangelisation, both by the Church of England and by the Roman Catholic Church. Both have relied on the quartet of Scripture, prayer, liturgy and the Sacraments. Most people consider that these campaigns have not been particularly successful. In this final chapter I respond to this disappointment by offering an alternative way forward.

We live in an age where relationships are considered the supreme expression of being human. Christianity has to recognise this reality by acknowledging that sanctification is to be found in the love present between people. This living intimacy reflects theologically the age of the supreme importance of the Trinity. The theology of the Trinity needs to be put on the map. Christianity has not seen this clearly or acknowledged it, because it believes that the world has lost its way by focusing exclusively on irresponsible sexual relationships. In fact, what the world is doing is searching for love, in and through the 'other', though it has yet to learn that love of the 'other' includes sex but is much more than that.

What is better suited to teach love and to put this truth on the map than Christianity, which is based on the Incarnation? So far, in the two thousand years of its existence, we have celebrated this truth of love principally in the Sacraments, especially in the Eucharist, and the word of God. Now we have to complete the love cycle. We have to apply a truth that lies innate in Christianity, that love is fulfilled in the fullness of the domestic church as described extensively in this book. Sacraments have not been a distraction, but a partial realisation of the truth of love. Believers have an awareness that love is to be found where Christ engages his life in the Church. Sacraments, particularly Baptism, Eucharist and Marriage, are recognised as sacred moments but we have to advance to the fullness of the sacred presence and its expression in all relationships which reflect the love that exists in the Trinity.

The world lives this truth in a shadowy, unclear way. Intuitively, it knows that there is something sacred about relationships. The task of Christianity has to be to penetrate the shadow and the mystery of this, and to live it out in loving relationships. This should be examined by everyone – theologians, lay men and women – for everyone can be a theologian. The theology of the domestic church is not my discovery. It has always been partially recognised. Psychology simply compels us to go one step further in a journey with the triune God.

Evangelisation through prayer, liturgy, the Sacraments and Scripture is like learning to talk. The domestic church, in faith and the living of love, is acquiring the correct and proper language of love, God's language. Both the ability to talk and the correct use of language are important. The history of Christianity is like the unfolding acquisition of the ability to speak the language of love. We start by learning rudimentary words, such as 'mama' or 'dada', and then continue to develop our language skills progressively through the unfolding life of the Church.

In prayer, Jesus called his Father, 'Abba', meaning 'Daddy', as a term of endearment. It is customarily held that prayer is a line of communication with God. It is in fact our line of communication of love: Christian life is both the spoken and the lived life of love. Evangelisation requires that Christianity understands and acknowledges this language of love in depth, not in a parrot-like fashion, not by rote, but in such depth that every thought, word and action between us, God and our neighbour authentically infiltrates and engages with the plurality of love. Love is a difficult language to acquire. We must not distort it through method learning, living it in Jung's terms as the Persona, or in Freud's terms as the False Self. In the Old Testament, Yahweh warned about the falsehood of burnt offerings. He wanted the authentic love of the heart. In the Church we must be careful not to substitute laws, rules and regulations for love.

Learning the language of love is very difficult. It is nothing less than learning the Kingdom of God. It is so difficult that we try to reduce it to a basic language, like the 'English in 500 words' which I learned at the age of 12. If we are not careful, we swallow up those 500 words in rules and regulations. The latter are useful but there is a danger of making them substitutes for real love, which requires nothing less than the Cross. Jesus' language of love to his Father and his relationship with him was a loving mature commitment, not an infantile dependence or obedience. In the Trinity he was coequal with the Father and the Spirit through relationships of love. This Trinitarian world of love is communicated to us in a variety of ways but particularly in the preface of John's Gospel, 'In the beginning was the Word.' The word of love allows us to speak to God and God to speak to us. For those who put their trust totally in the word of God in the Scriptures, especially in sexual matters, it is important to realise that, unless the word is embedded in and interpreted by love, it is not the full word of God, but a human projection, embellished with a large measure of historically conditioned prejudice. This is particularly important in the current debate over homosexuality.

For evangelisation, love is the bridge between Christianity and the world. The world and even the Churches' own adherents may not trust the Churches but everyone trusts genuine love because, however wounded we are in our personalities, we all have a sense of what it means and we hunger for it. When Christianity makes the fact that God is love its priority, puts it on the map, preaches it year in year out and makes it the centre of its life, not only in abstract words but in living love, we will have the key to evangelisation.

Love is the international language of God. It is, of course, the most difficult reality to discern and live but that is the primary task both of Judaism and Christianity. That, in my opinion, is what all the Churches that claim apostolic descent are there to do, and particularly the Roman Catholic Church with its special claim. I write, of course, as a Roman Catholic but I live the hope that ecumenically we can all work for the discernment of love, and particularly with our Jewish friends from whom we have a lot to learn about the centrality of love in the home.

We criticise the world for its consumerism, materialism, hedonism and so on. The world remains unhappy because money, goods and possessions are not substitutes for peace and happiness. As a psychiatrist, I have seen this reality throughout my professional life. Christianity makes the mistake of attacking this materialism and consumerism. We will not convert the world by attacking it. We will only evangelise when we seek to sell love not goods. How many sermons do we preach purely on love (even though the word is frequently there)? How many sermons do we preach on marital love, the love of kinship, the love of friendship, the love of the body and sexuality?

If Jesus prayed to his Father in and through love, we can do no better than imitate him. There is clearly a place for prayers of petition, thanksgiving, worship and celebration. We recognise and pray the prayer of love with our bodies in marriage, in sexual intercourse, in the celebration of kinship, in the intimacy of friendship, in the love of furthering creation through work and in many other concrete ways. I have referred before to the fact that love is mentioned frequently in our liturgies: we sing about it in hymns, but we find it very difficult to live it in practice. We find it even more difficult to grasp it theologically than in its living reality. This book is a plea to advance this concept and for Christianity to extol and facilitate its living.

I finish not by criticism or condemnation of the world. If it fails in love, much of the responsibility is ours as men and women of God. Our responsibility is to point out the heresies of our age against intimate relationships of love: first, marital breakdown, with its enormous betrayal of love; secondly, any child, for whatever reason apart from death, being brought up without two loving parents; thirdly, disposable relationships of any type. There are, of course, many others but I mention these three leading ones that between them are mainly responsible for betraying love. I do not condemn or criticise single parents, the divorced, those whose relationships go wrong, and who feel unloveable and make a mess of their lives. I do not join the favourite pastime of labelling all these people as 'sinners'. As a psychiatrist I know better.

One of the reasons why the world will not trust the Churches is that they see us as hypocrites. In this, they are not always fair, but the gap between proclaiming love and living it is a constant danger for Christians, indeed for everyone who aspires to love. That is why the Cross is necessary. The answer to these modern heresies is not more anathemas. What we need is prayer, faith, love and the funds for adequate, ongoing research and training in order to understand and prevent these problems.

What I plead is for all those who adhere to the Judaeo-Christian tradition and all people of good will to work and think constantly how to reduce the gap of hypocrisy between aspired and lived love, and to make the reduction of this gap their priority. I also believe this is the answer to the withdrawal from religious practice. In past ages, discerning fundamental Christian truths and constructing orthodoxies and credos were priorities. In the light of the psychosocial discoveries of the last hundred years or so, I now make a plea for our age to work on the orthodoxy and the construction of credos for living love, a task for all of us. Safeguarding the dignity of the person should be the first priority for the Judaeo-Christian tradition. Ensuring that life is love in its living form is no less important because, when that happens, we have the anticipated love of the next world.

My conclusion is that all Christianity, but particularly Roman Catholicism, is split into two halves, an older generation who still follow the traditional identity of the Church and a younger, much larger group who are abandoning this tradition in large numbers, mistrust the Churches, but are still seeking to find God. This requires a radical solution, and my hope is that the whole of Christianity will find it in a living love which penetrates its whole life. It cannot go wrong because God is love.

References

Preface
1. Dominian, J., *Christian Marriage* (Darton, Longman and Todd, 1967).
2. Dominian, J., *Let's Make Love* (Darton, Longman and Todd, 2002).

Part One: The Church Today

1: The Decline of the Traditional Churches
1. Heald, G., 'Where have all the Catholics Gone?', *The Tablet*, 19 June 1999.
2. Heald, G. and Judd, G., 'The Soul of Britain', *The Tablet*, 3 June 2000.
3. Heald, G., 'Where have all the Catholics Gone?'.
4. ibid.
5. *Population Studies*, First marriages for both parties 1990 (209,000), 2001 (156,000) (HMSO, 2000).
6. Heald, G., 'Where have all the Catholics Gone?'.
7. Gibson, D., *The Coming Catholic Church* (HarperSanFrancisco, 2003).
8. ibid., p. 78.
9. ibid., p. 79.
10. ibid., p. 79.
11. The statistical data from Canada is taken from three sources, the book *Restless Gods* (Stoddart, 2002), by the influential religious sociologist, Reginald W. Bibby, who has been doing national surveys in Canada for nearly thirty years, the 2001 census of Religions in Canada, and research by Novalis, the publishers.
12. Bibby, *Restless Gods*.
13. ibid., p. 30.
14. ibid., p. 31.
15. ibid., p. 31.

References

2: The Emergence of a New Spirituality
1. Hughes, G. W., *God in All Things* (Hodder and Stoughton, 2003), ch. 21.

3: Redefining the Identity of the Church
1. Pius XII, *Mystici Corporis*, 1943.

4: The Persistent Sense of God
1. Heald, G. and Judd, G., *BBC Soul of Britain* (Orb, 2000).
2. Feuerbach, L. A., *The Essence of Christianity* (Harper, 1854, new ed. 1957).
3. Hardy, A., *The Spiritual Nature of Man* (Clarendon Press, 1979).
4. Hay, D. and Hunt, K., *Understanding the Spiritual Nature of People who Don't go to Church* (Centre for the Study of Human Relations, 2000).

5: Autonomy, Authority and Trust
1. Barker, D., in *Governance and Authority in the Roman Catholic Church*, N. Tims and K. Wilson (eds) (SPCK, 2000).

6: Sexuality
1. See Dominian, J., *Let's Make Love* (Darton, Longman and Todd, 2001), for a fuller account of the history of sexuality in the Church in the last 2000 years.
2. Luther, 'Hochzeit predigt on Heb. XIII', *C. Werke* (e) 111.
3. Sipe, R., *A Secret World: Sexuality and the Search for Celibacy* (Brunner/Mazel, 1990).
4. Bauman, Z., *Liquid Love* (Polity Press, 2003).
5. Durkin, M. G., *Feast of Love: John Paul II on human intimacy* (Loyola University Press, 1983).
6. Thatcher, A., *Living Together and Christian Ethics*, (Cambridge University Press, 2002).

Part Two: The Concept of Love

8: The Centrality of God
1. Bauman, Z., *Liquid Love* (Polity Press, 2003).

9: The Psychology of Love
1. Gomez, L., *An Introduction to Object Relations* (Free Association Books, 1998).

10: Intimate Relationships in Childhood and Adulthood
1. Ainsworth, M. D. S., Blehar, M. C. and Walls, S., *Patterns of Attachment: a psychological study of the stranger situation* (Lawrence Erlbaum, Hillsdale, 1997).

References

2. Piaget, J., *Origins of Intelligence in the Child* (Routledge and Keegan Paul, 1953).
3. Kohlberg, L., *The Meaning and Measurement of Moral Development* (Clark University Press, 1981)

11: Marriage: a Loving Community
1. Dominian, J., *Christian Marriage* (Darton, Longman and Todd, 1967), p. 243.
2. Abbott, W. M., *Pastoral Constitution in the World* (Chapman, 1967), Part II, ch. I.
3. John Paul II, *The Theology of the Body – Human Love in the Divine Plan* (Pauline Books and Media, 1997).
4. Durkin, M. G., *Feast of Love: John Paul II on Human Intimacy* (Loyola University Press, 1983).
5. ibid.

Part Three: Marriage and the Family

12: Falling in Love and Loving
1. A recent and very good book on love is Armstrong, J., *The Conditions of Love* (Penguin, 2002).
2. Klinger, E., *Meaning and Void: inner experiences and incentives in people's lives* (University of Minnesota, 1977).
3. Campbell, A., Couvaise, P. E. and Rogers, W. L., *The Quality of American Life* (Russell Sage Foundation, 1976).
4. Dominian, J., *Marriage, Faith and Love* (Darton, Longman and Todd, 1981).

14: Healing and Growth
1. Abbott, W. M., *Documents of Vatican II: The Church Today* (Geoffrey Chapman, 1967), Part II, ch. I.

15: Sexual Intercourse
1. Dominian, J., *Let's Make Love: the meaning of sexual intercourse* (Darton, Longman and Todd, 2001).
2. Durkin, M. G., *Feast of Love: John Paul II on human intimacy* (Loyola University Press, 1983).
3. Abbott, W. M., *Documents of Vatican II:* Gaudium et Spes (Geoffrey Chapman, 1967), Part II, ch. I.
4. Durkin, *Feast of Love.*
5. Dominian, *Let's Make Love.*

19: Education for Sexuality
1. Wellings, K. et al., *Sexual Behaviour in Britain* (Penguin, 1994).
2. *Social Exclusion Unity* (HMSO, 1999).
3. Wellings, *Sexual Behaviour in Britain*.
4. ibid.
5. Thatcher, A., *Living Together and Christian Ethics* (Cambridge University Press, 2002).
6. ibid.
7. Bauman, Z., *Liquid Love* (Polity, 2003).

20: What Happens When a Marriage Breaks Down?
1. Hornsby-Smith, M. P. et al., *Patterns of Religious Commitment, Intermarriage and Marital Breakdown among English Catholics* (Archives de Science Sociale des Religion, 64/1, 1987).
2. Kelly, K. T., *Divorce and Second Marriages – Facing the Challenge* (Geoffrey Chapman, 1996).
3. Haring, B., *No Way Out? Pastoral Care of the Divorced and Remarried* (St Paul's Publications, 1989).
4. Buckley, T. J., *What Binds Marriage?* (Chapman, London, 1997).
5. Dominian, J., 'The Christian Response to Marital Breakdown', *Ampleforth Journal*, Spring 1968.

21: The Family: a Domestic Church
1. Luther, 'Hochzeitpredigt on Heb. XIII', *C.Werke* (e) XXI.
2. Dominian, J., *Marriage, Faith and Love* (Darton, Longman and Todd, 1981).
3. Dominian, J., *Let's Make Love* (Darton, Longman and Todd, 2001).
4. Abbott, W. M., *The Documents of Vatican II* (Geoffrey Chapman, 1967).
5. ibid. OR John Paul II, *Familiaris Consortio* (Catholic Truth Society, 1981).

Part Four: The Wider Family

22: Kinship
1. Ikkink, K. K. et al., 'Perceived Instrumental Support Exchanges in Relationships between Elderly Parents and their Adult Children', *Journal of Marriage and the Family*, vol. 61, no. 4, 1999.
2. Ciccirelli, V. G., 'Sibling Relationships in Cross-cultural Perspectives', *Journal of Marriage and the Family*, vol. 56, no. 1, 1994.
3. ibid.
4. Stein, C. H. et al., 'Because they are my Parents', *Journal of Marriage and the Family*, vol. 60, no. 3, 1998.
5. *Social Trends*, no. 31 (HMSO, ?).

References

23: Friendship
1. Stuart, E., *Just Good Friends* (Mowbray, 1995).
2. Aelred, *Spiritual Friendship* (Cistercian Publications, 1974), 1. 54–5.
3. Aelred, *The Mirror of Charity* 3, cited in Boswell, J., *Christianity, Social Tolerance and Homosexuality* (?, 1980).
4. Stuart, *Just Good Friends.*

24: Singleness
1. Argyle, M., *The Psychology of Interpersonal Behaviour* (Penguin, 1994).
2. Davies, D. L., *British Journal of Preventive and Social Medicine*, vol. 10, 1956.
3. McAllister, F., *Marital Breakdown: the Health of the Nation* (One Plus One, 1995, second edition).
4. Bowlby, J., *Attachment and Loss* (Basic Books, 1969), vol. 1; *Attachment and Loss: Separation Anxiety and Anger* (Basic Books, 1973) vol. 2; *Attachment and Loss: Sadness and Depression* (Basic Books, 1980), vol. 3.
5. Parkes, C. M., *Bereavement: Studies of Grief in Adult Life* (Taylor and Francis, 2001).

25: Religious Life
1. Cozzens, D. B., *The Changing Face of the Priesthood* (The Liturgical Press, 2000).
2. Dominian, J., *Let's Make Love: the meaning of sexual intercourse* (Darton, Longman and Todd, 2001).
3. John Paul II, *Familiaris Consortio* (Catholic Truth Society, 1981).

26: Work
1. John Paul II, *Laborem exercens: the Encyclicals of John Paul II* (Sunday Visitor, 1981).
2. Greene, M., *Thank God It's Monday* (Scripture Union, 1997).
3. Greene, M., 'Supporting Christians at Work', *How to Guide* (London Institute for Contemporary Christianity, 2001), vol. 2, no 6.
4. One Plus One

27: Loving Ourselves and Our Neighbours
1. Palmer, M., *Freud and Jung on Religion* (Routledge, 1997).
2. Dominian, J., *One Like Us: a Psychological Interpretation of Jesus* (Darton, Longman and Todd, 1998).

28: Two Churches: the Domestic and the Local
1. Abbott W. M., *The Documents of Vatican II* (Geoffrey Chapman, 1967).

Index

Index

celebration 134, 136, 144, 193
celibacy 12, 32, 38–9, 46–7, 75, 137, 170
Centre for the Study of Human Relations 28
childbirth 135, 137–8
childhood 68–72, 84, 87–8, 90, 94
children 3, 8, 23–4, 70, 73, 84, 86
church attendance 2–3, 7–9, 11–12, 22
Church of England 8, 137
Church Tribunals 133
Cicero 150
Code of Canon Law 133
cognition 70–2, 94
cohabitation 128, 156, 158–9, 163, 183
Communal Reconciliation 46–7
communication 86–9, 91, 99, 104–5, 120–1, 153
Communion 132, 135, 192
Confession 8, 31, 46–7
Confirmation 9, 135, 192
conflict resolution 86, 90–1, 99, 105
Consecration 44, 45
Constantine, Emperor 21, 51, 71
contraception 21, 31, 45, 75–6, 100
conversion 9, 59
counselling 60, 84, 89, 91–2, 161, 190, 196
Curia 24, 31–2, 46, 73

Darwin, C. 27
defence mechanisms 58–60, 187–8, 195
denial 58–9
dependence 131
depression 135, 158–60, 162, 179, 187, 189
discipline 121–3, 177
divorce 15, 75, 83, 87, 89, 130–6
domestic church 137–42, 170, 180, 191–4
Durkin, M. 76–7

Eastern religions 16
education 111, 113, 116–18, 134
Electra complex 58
encyclicals 15, 18–19, 22–3, 38
engagement neurosis 157
Enlightenment 27, 30
environment 16, 17
envy 163, 165, 183
ethology 66
Eucharist 8, 24, 34, 44, 46, 62
European Values Survey 35–6
euthanasia 15, 16
evangelisation 198–202

Fairbairn, R. 60–1, 64–5, 70, 81, 86–7, 164, 187
Fall 150
falling in love 81–3, 126–7
family 137–42, 168, 179–80, 188
feminism 152
Feuerbach, L. A. 28
First Vatican Council 30
forgiveness 85, 100, 103–10, 112, 130, 187
fornication 124, 135
free association 57
Freud, S. 37, 40, 56–65, 84
friendship 3, 71, 84, 87

gender 152
Godhead 101
'good enough' mothers 63, 177
Good Samaritan 53, 186
grace 51, 73, 92, 139–40, 148
grandparents 147–8
greed 16, 122
Greek Orthodox Church 132–3
Greeks 113, 185
Greene, M. 172, 177
growth 85, 90, 92, 96–103, 107, 110

Hardy, A. 28, 29
Hay, D. 28
healing 16, 69, 85, 92–105, 110
health 177

Index

hierarchy 14, 20–1, 115–16, 152, 175, 194
Hinduism 16, 163
Homer 149, 150
homosexuality 10, 76, 100, 138
Humanae Vitae 74–5, 99, 101–2
Hume, Cardinal 35, 139

identification 59
incest 68, 183
individuation 96, 184–5
internalisation 120
International Conference of the Teams of Our Lady 85
intimate relationships 68–72, 83–4
Ireland 167
Islam 16

John Paul II, Pope 12, 18, 20–1, 24
John XXIII, Pope 35
Judaeo-Christian tradition 27, 29, 51, 200, 202
Jung, C. G. 28–9, 56, 84, 86, 96

Kierkegaard, S. 151
Kinsey, A. C. 40
kinship 3, 84, 113, 117, 143–8
Klein, M. 61–3, 122
Klinger, E. 83–4
Kohlberg, L. 70, 113–14, 185

laity 2–3, 8, 19–20, 23–4, 32–3

Last Judgement 150
Last Supper 44
Latin 21, 31, 44, 167
laziness 119
leadership 10, 114
liberals 34, 35
libido 58, 64, 86, 100, 124, 164, 187
listening 88, 104, 121, 179, 186–8
liturgy 2–3, 7, 14, 17, 37, 42
loneliness 163–4
Luther, M. 38, 137

Magisterium 15, 18, 20, 24, 31–3
marginalisation 15, 121, 135
marriage 8, 10, 23, 32, 34, 39–40
    breakdown 130–6
    love 53, 83–4, 86–91, 183
    sexuality 99–102, 125, 127
martyrs 16, 70, 112
Marx, K. 28
Mass 7–9, 11, 21, 44–6, 140, 167, 192
Masters and Johnson 40
masturbation 164
maturation 181
maturity 111–23, 131, 166–9
media 37–8, 111
medicine 16
mental illness 158, 166–7
Methodists 8
Milne, L. 144
monasteries 168, 192
money 180, 200
monotheism 27
Montaigne, M. E. de 151
Morrow, D. 178

nature versus nurture 61, 93, 121
neighbours 181–90
neuroses 56–7
New Age movement 17
New Testament 45, 52–3, 125, 128, 138, 173
Nichols, Archbishop V. 18
Nonconformists 8
Nottingham University 28

Object Relations theory 56, 60–7, 70
Ocean Synod of Bishops 15
Oedipus complex 58, 183
Old Testament 28, 38, 45, 51–2
One Plus One 178
one-night stands 108–9, 129
ordinations 8, 167

papal infallibility 30

211

Index

touch 63, 66, 82, 88–9, 108, 121
transference 57, 60, 94, 188–9, 195
Transfiguration 105
transitional objects 64
Trent, Council of 30, 138
Trinity 3, 41, 51, 101, 155
trust 18–19, 30–6, 41, 69–70, 108–10
truth 119

unconscious 57–8, 60, 65, 94
United States of America (USA) 9–12, 113

Vatican 9–10, 30

Vatican II 2–3, 19–25, 30–4, 36, 40–1, 44–6, 47, 73–4, 81, 83, 92, 98, 99, 101–2, 112, 116–117, 125, 137–40, 151, 166, 168–70, 174, 191–2, 194, 195
violence 122
vocation 166–8

weddings 138, 192
Winnicott, D. 61, 63–4, 88, 94, 176
withdrawal 91, 127, 161
women priests 10, 138
work 3, 37, 87, 104, 112, 135, 147, 153, 166, 172–80, 194
wounds 93–5, 97, 103, 105–6, 110, 187